Doctor Mozart® Music Theor

MW00380735

In-Depth Piano Theory Fun for Music Lessons and Home Schooling

Level 2C - Contents

2 ....Octaves and Unisons
3 ....Italian Musical Terms
4 ....White Key Enharmonics Review
5-6 ....Interval Review
7-10 .....Scales and Key Signatures
11 ....What is a Key?
12 ....Triad Test
13-14 ...Interval Challenge
15-17 ...Natural Minor Scales
18 ....Key Signature Quiz
19-20 ...Interval Inversions
21-24 ...6ths and 7ths
25-28 ...Interval Practice
29 ....Triad Quiz
30-32 ...Harmonic Minor Scales
33 ....Dotted Quarter Notes
34-36 ...16th Notes and Rests
37-38 ...Review: Scales and Triads
39 ....Certificate of Achievement

Every day, start by reviewing what you learned the day before. Then complete a page or two, and you will make good progress.

Highly Effective for Children Learning a Musical Instrument.

Doctor Mozart workbooks are filled with friendly cartoon characters. They make it fun to learn music theory in-depth. And in-depth music theory knowledge is essential for children learning a musical instrument. Use Doctor Mozart workbooks by themselves or with other teaching materials. Use them for music lessons and for home schooling.

The authors, Machiko and Paul Musgrave, are both graduates of Juilliard. Machiko has taught piano and theory at Soai University in Japan. Paul is an Associate of the Royal Conservatory of Music. The authors hope you enjoy using this book!

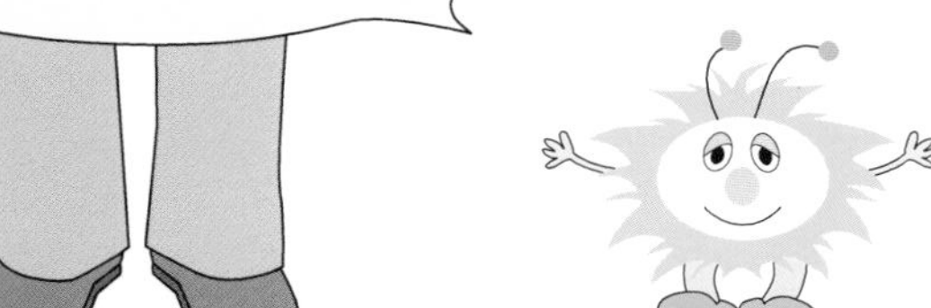

Copyright laws protect the right of authors and publishers to earn a living from their work. Please respect these laws, and pay for the books you use and enjoy. Photocopying or reproducing this book in any manner may lead to prosecution.

Many thanks to Kevin Musgrave for his meticulous proof-reading and insightful suggestions.
Created by Machiko and Paul Christopher Musgrave. Illustrated by Machiko Yamane Musgrave.
Version 1.0.5

Doctor Mozart Music Theory Workbook, Level 2C. © MMVIII, MMXIII Machiko and Paul Christopher Musgrave. Published by April Avenue Music. www.DoctorMozart.com 800 567-8878

Octaves and Unisons

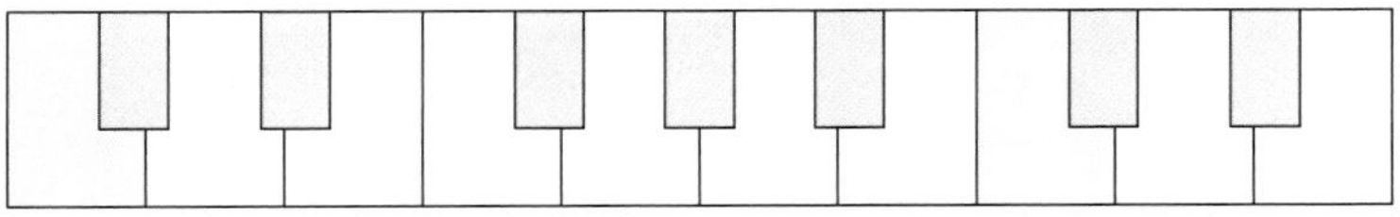

The two pink keys are 8 notes apart. They form an octave, or P8.

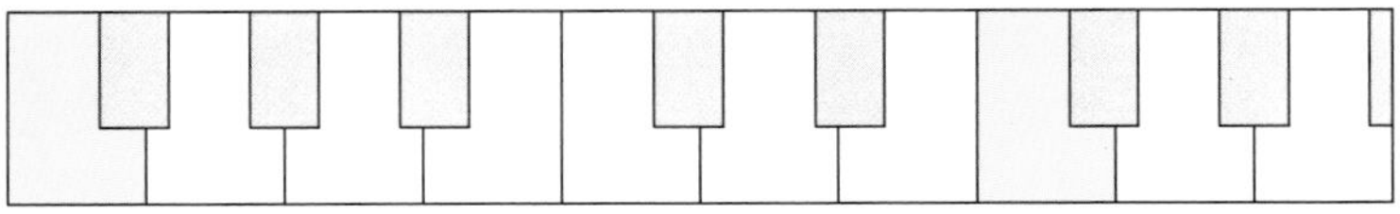

Are the two green keys one octave apart? ______
The symbol for octave is ___8.

An octave is an interval that spans ____ alphabet letters on the keyboard. Circle each pair of letters that could form an octave:

C C   G A   B♭ B♭   H H   F♯ F♯

Octaves are perfect, not major.
P8
Octave = P8

Name the following notes. Then write notes in between to make octaves.

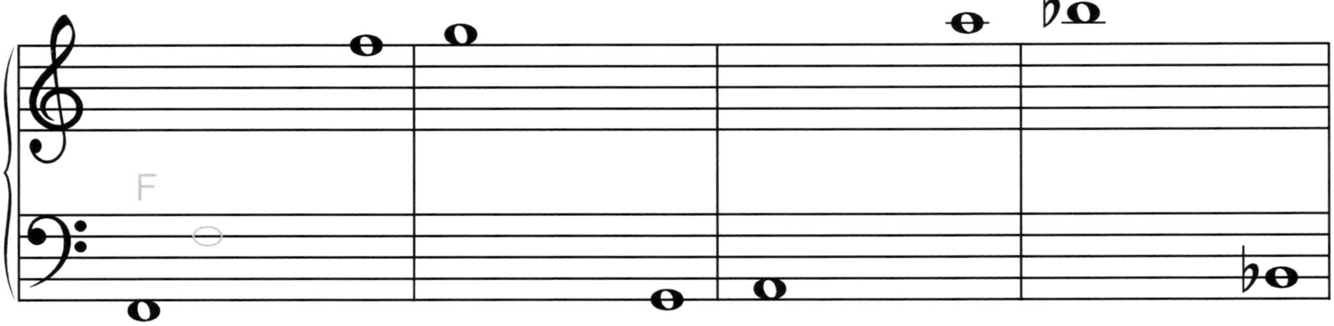
F

Name these intervals.

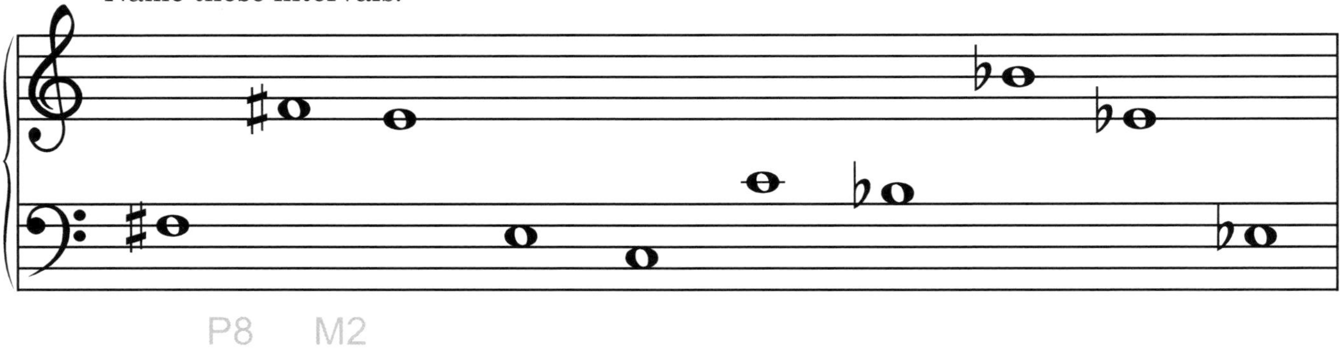
P8
M2

Unison = P1
P1

What is a unison? If two instruments play the same note at the same time, then we say they are playing a unison. Below, write several unisons and octaves. Use some accidentals. When writing unisons, write the two notes *beside* each other.

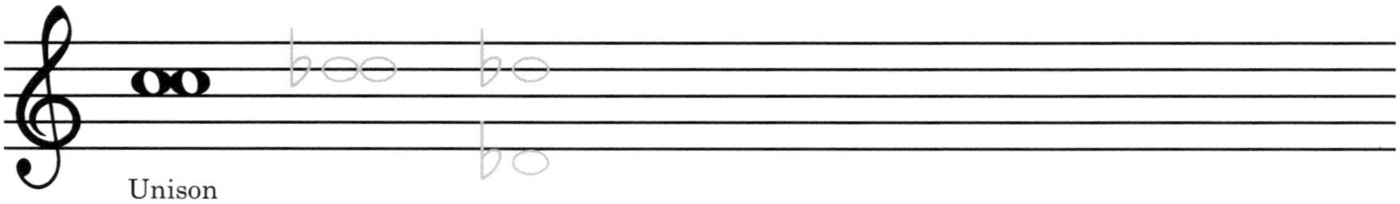

Unison
P1

The symbol for perfect unison is P1.

 © MMVIII, MMXIII Machiko and Paul Christopher Musgrave. Published by April Avenue Music. www.DoctorMozart.com 800 567-8878

Italian Musical Terms

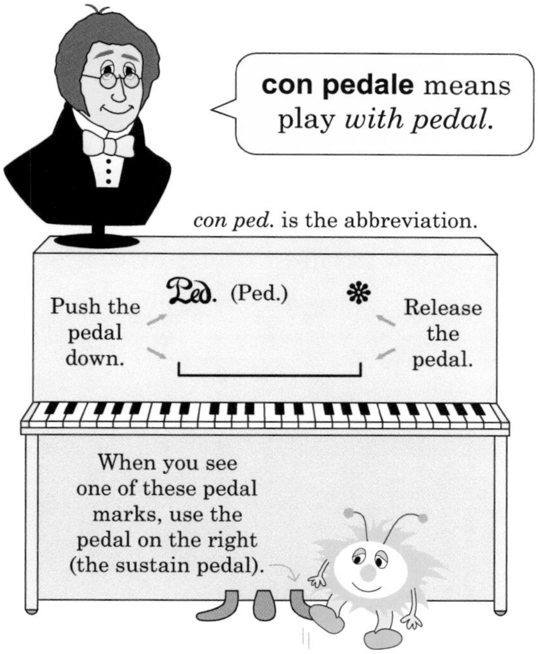
con pedale means play *with pedal.*
con ped. is the abbreviation.
Push the pedal down.
Ped. (Ped.)
✻
Release the pedal.
When you see one of these pedal marks, use the pedal on the right (the sustain pedal).

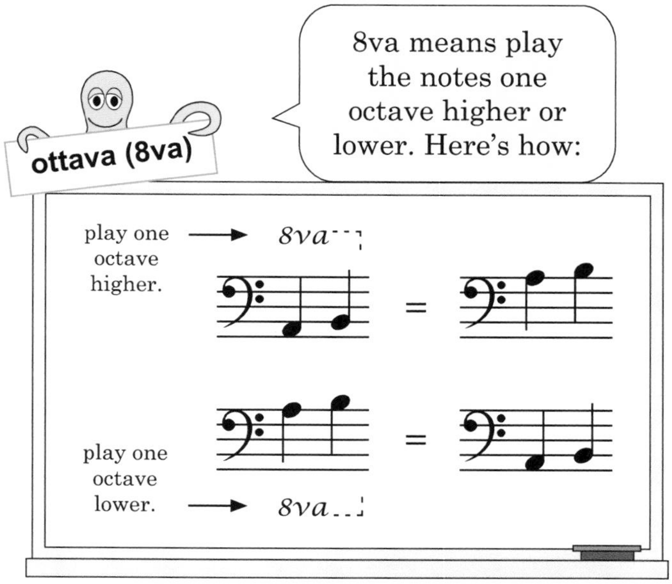
ottava (8va)
8va means play the notes one octave higher or lower. Here's how:
play one octave higher.
8va
=
play one octave lower.
8va

8va is short for *ottava*, which is Italian for *octave*.

mano sinistra
M.S.
left hand
M.D.
right hand
mano destra

A *tenuto* sign (–) tells you to hold the note for its full normal duration, or slightly longer.
tenuto
Trace.

The abbreviation for tenuto is *ten.*

Write a word or sign in each blank.

The Italian word for octave: ______________

Hold the note for its full length: ___________

Use the sustain pedal: con_______________

Play with your right hand: M._____

Play with your left hand: _______

Do these pedal marks Ped. ✻ have the same meaning as this pedal mark? ⌊____⌋ _______

Next, look at the signs. Then write the actual notes on the lower staff.

8va
8va
8va
8va

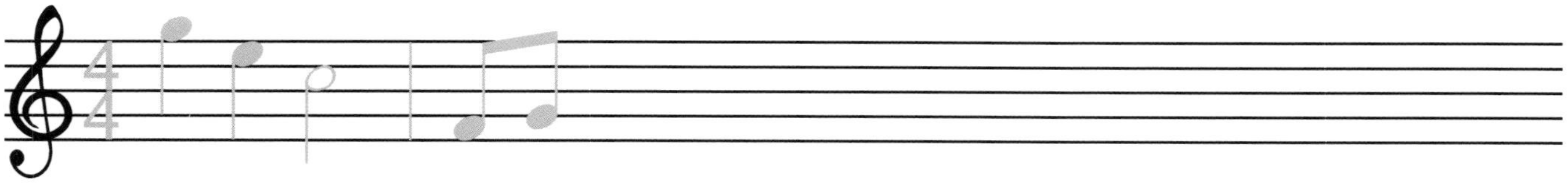

Doctor Mozart Music Theory Workbook, Level 2C. © MMVIII, MMXIII Machiko and Paul Christopher Musgrave. Published by April Avenue Music. www.DoctorMozart.com 800 567-8878

White keys!
Level 2B review

White key
Enharmonics

We have two names each.

In the colored boxes, name each key two different ways. Write the notes on the staff. Draw lines.

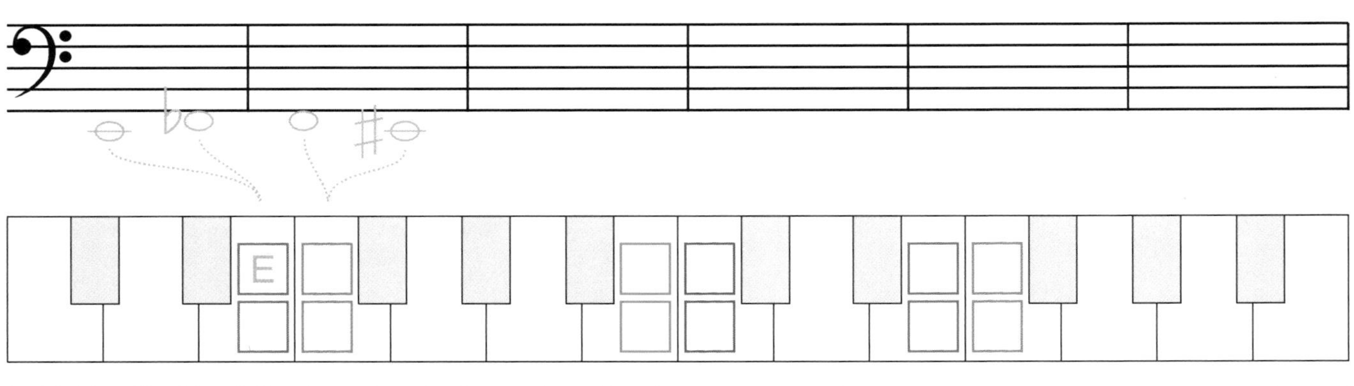
E

Draw lines from the printed notes to the keys. In the empty bars, write the enharmonic equivalents. Then draw lines from the new notes to the keyboard.

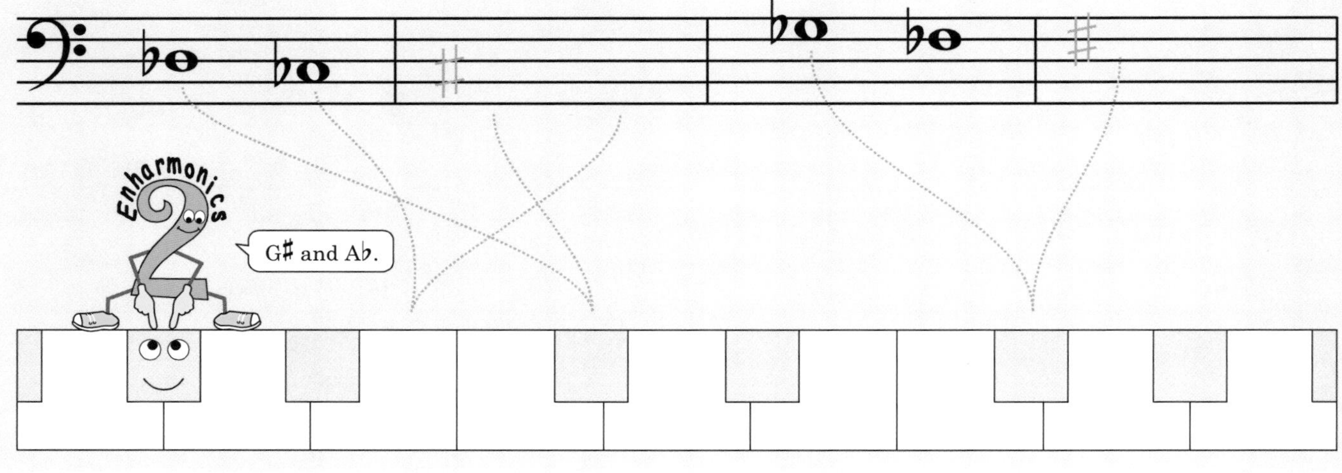
Enharmonics
G♯ and A♭.

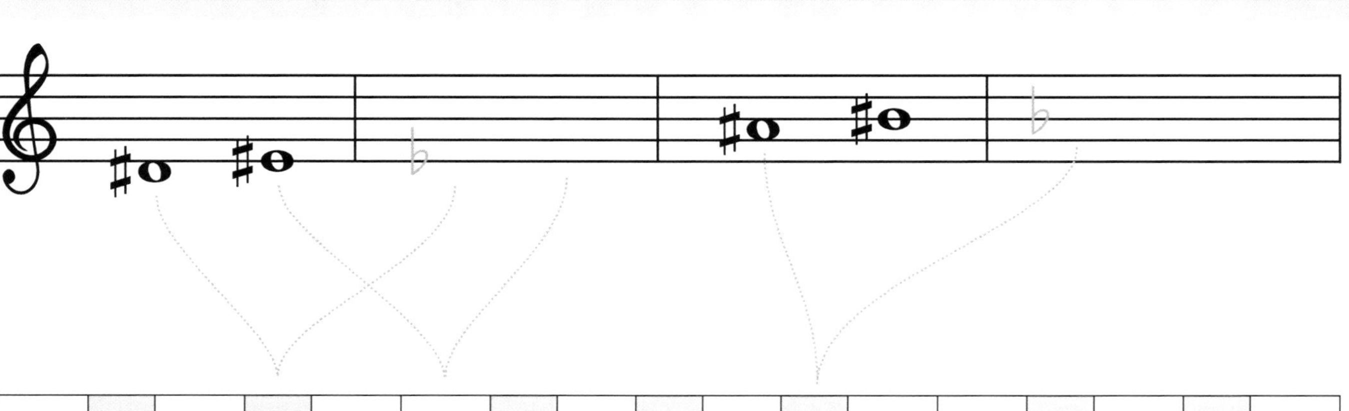

  Published by April Avenue Music. www.DoctorMozart.com 800 567-8878

Interval Review

Write neighboring alphabet letters in the boxes. For each interval, label the white keys first, then the black keys. Draw a square bracket at each whole step. Draw a V bracket at each half step. Name the intervals.

m2
M2
m3
M3
P4
Cats & Dogs Chess Co.

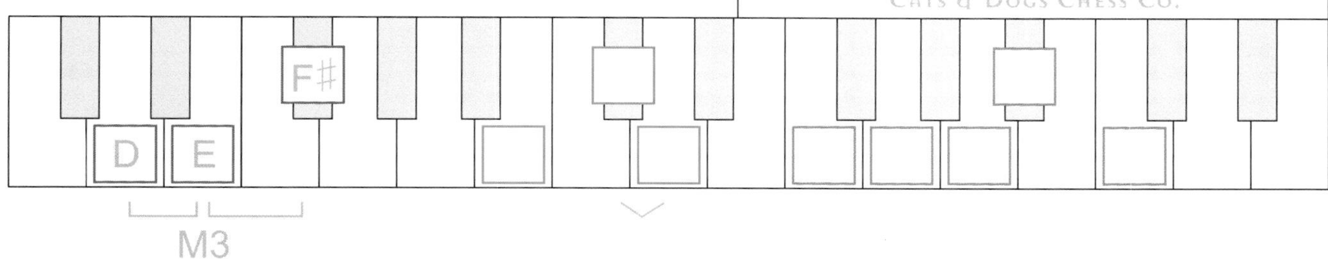
F♯
D
E
M3

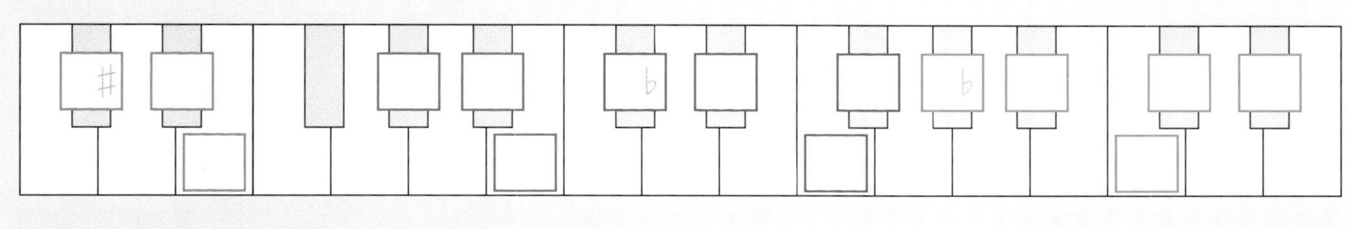
♯
♭
♭

How many letter names does each of these intervals span? m2 2 M2 ___ m3 ___ M3 ___ P4 ___

Name the keys to show the intervals. Start at each labeled key, and go up. Draw brackets.

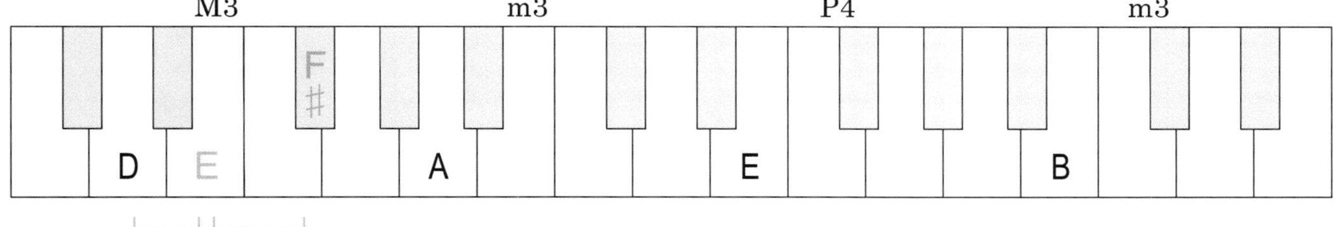
M3
m3
P4
m3
F♯
D
E
A
E
B

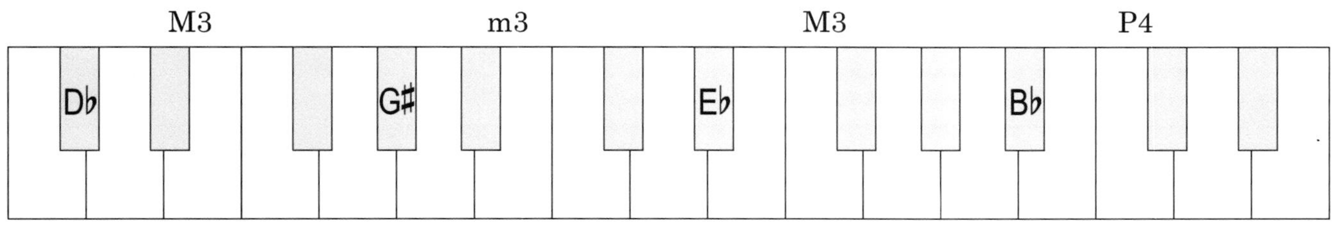
M3
m3
M3
P4
D♭
G♯
E♭
B♭

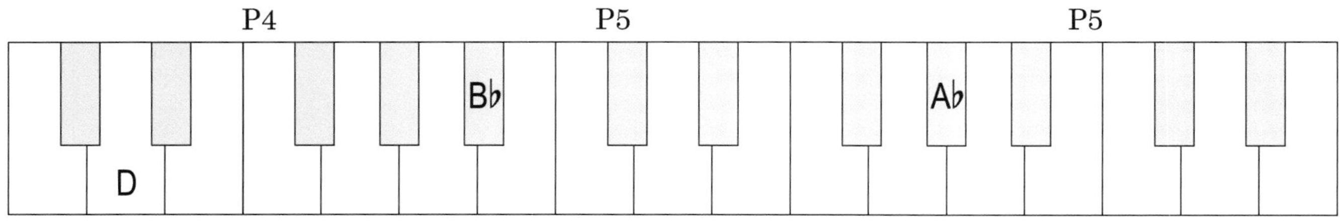
P4
P5
P5
B♭
A♭
D

Review from level 2B

Black Key Intervals

Name the intervals.
Draw lines to the keyboard.

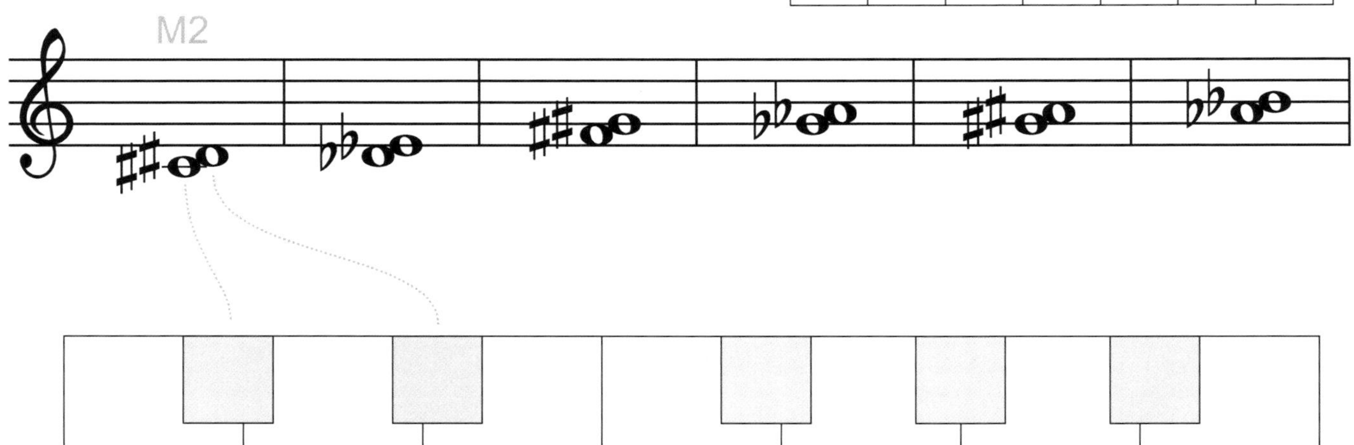
M2

On this staff, write a harmonic M2 above each given note. Draw lines.

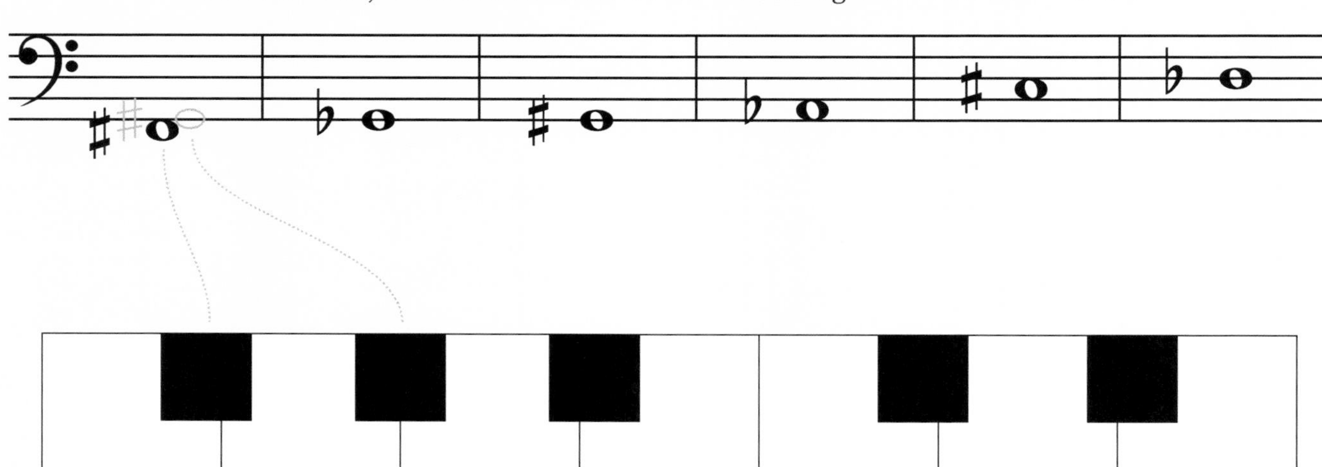

Write a harmonic interval above each note, as indicated. Draw lines.

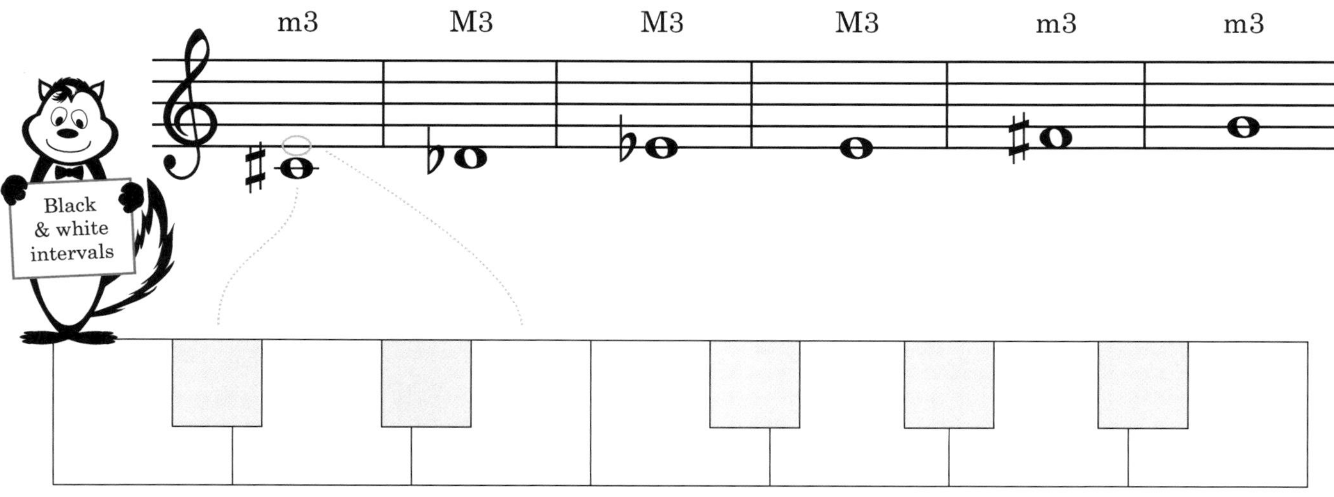
m3
M3
M3
M3
m3
m3
Black & white intervals

  Published by April Avenue Music. www.DoctorMozart.com 800 567-8878

The D Major Scale and Primary Triads

The Roman numerals on this keyboard show a D Major scale.
Draw square and V brackets. Which keys are black? _____ and _____

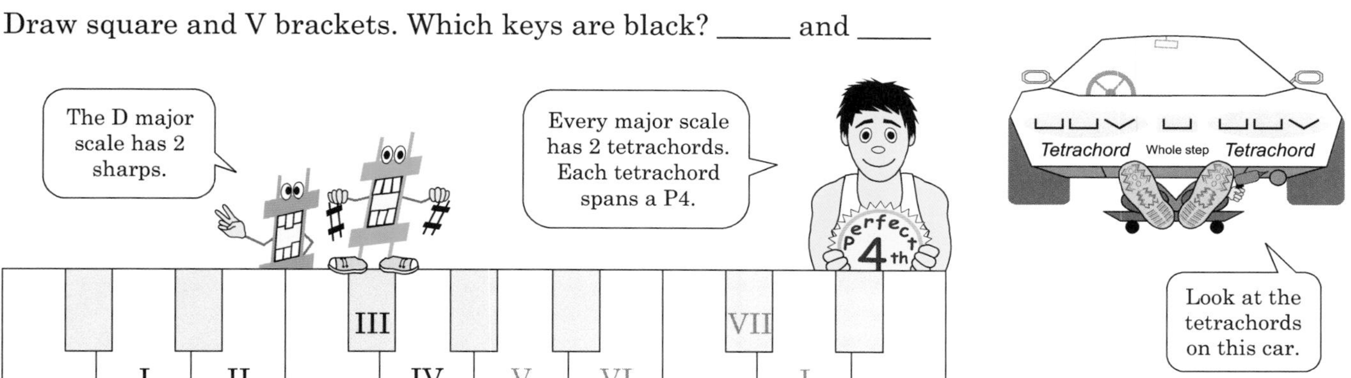

The D major scale has 2 sharps.
Every major scale has 2 tetrachords. Each tetrachord spans a P4.
Perfect 4th
Tetrachord
Whole step
Tetrachord
Look at the tetrachords on this car.
I
II
III
IV
V
VI
VII
I

Write a triad on I, IV, and V. Draw square and V brackets. Draw lines.

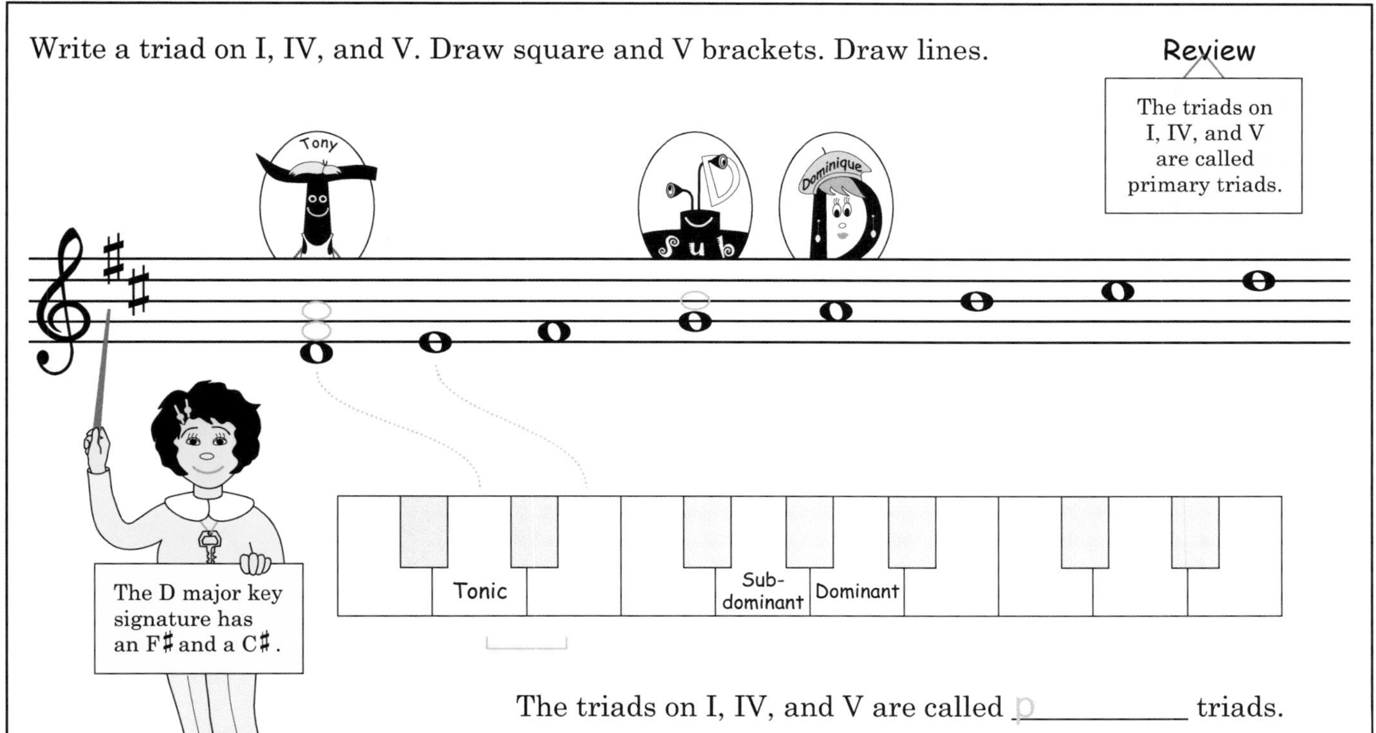

Review
The triads on I, IV, and V are called primary triads.
Tony
Sub
Dominique
Tonic
Sub-dominant
Dominant
The D major key signature has an F♯ and a C♯.

The triads on I, IV, and V are called p__________ triads.

On the staff below, write a D major key signature. Write an ascending D major scale. Write the primary triads. Draw lines from the scale notes to the keys.

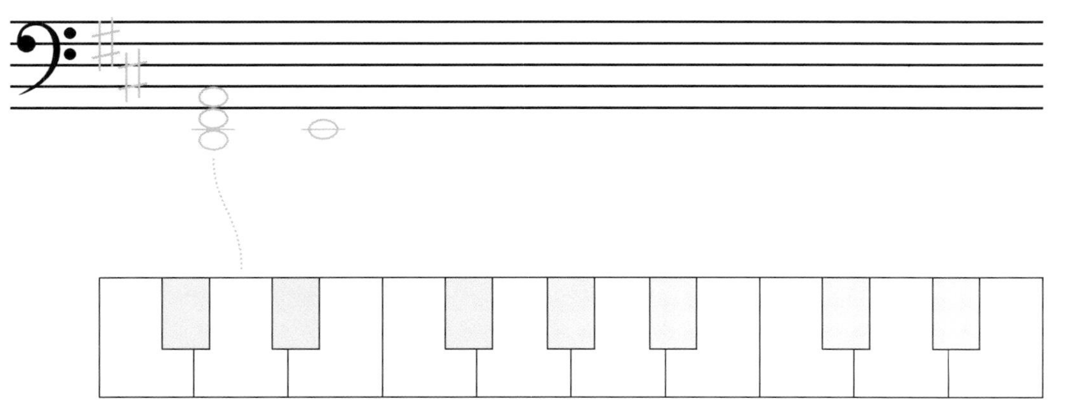

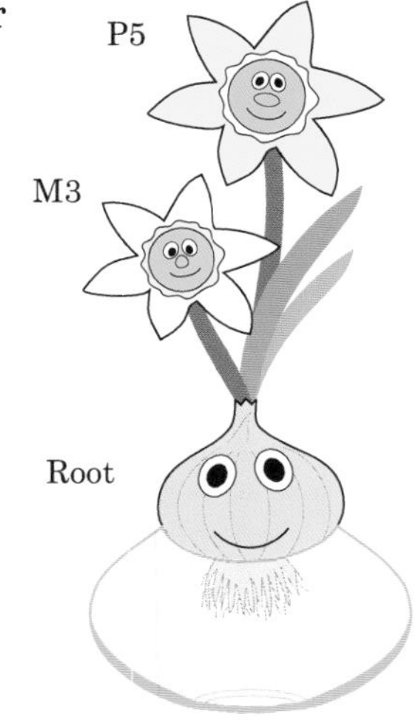

P5
M3
Root

  Published by April Avenue Music. www.DoctorMozart.com 800 567-8878

The B Flat Major Scale and Primary Triads

The B flat major scale has 2 flats.

Draw square and V brackets for this scale.
Which keys are black? _____ and _____.
The name of this scale is ___________ major.

Every major scale has 2 tetrachords. Each tetrachord spans a P4.

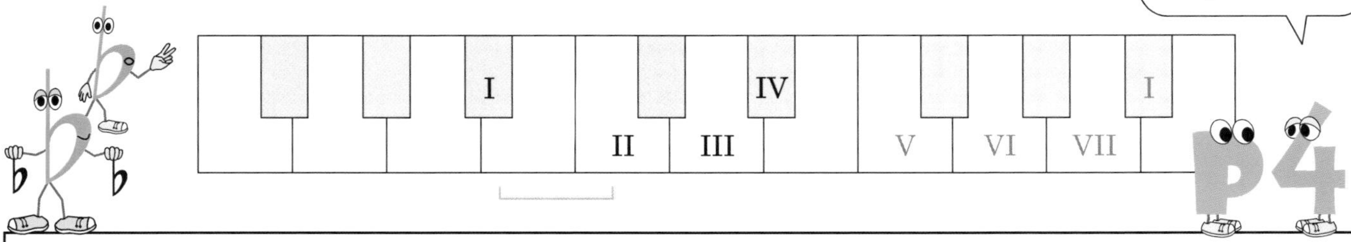

I II III IV V VI VII I

P4

The B♭ major key signature has a B♭ and an E♭.

Write an ascending B flat major scale.
Draw brackets and lines.
Write the primary triads.

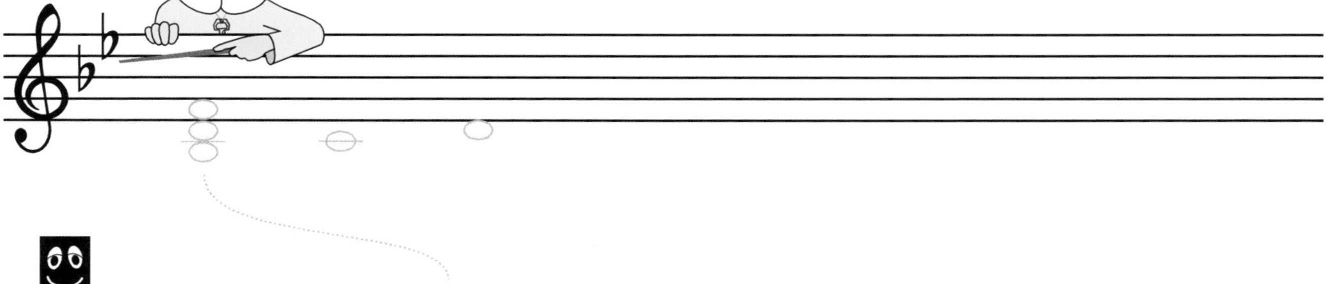

The tonic note is a black key.

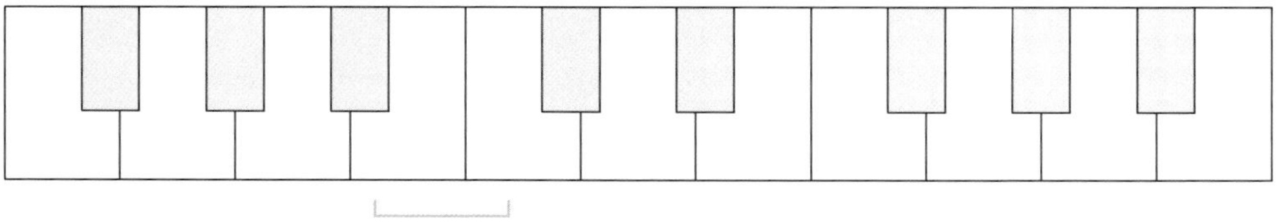

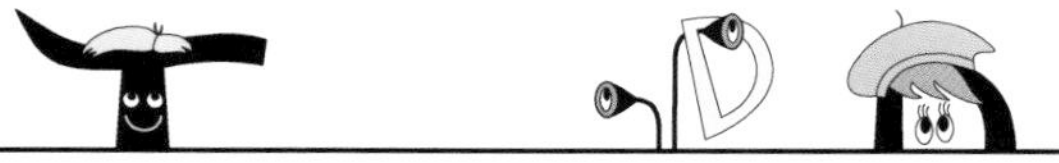

Each tetrachord spans a ___4.

Write a B flat major key signature and scale on the staff. Write the primary triads. Draw lines.

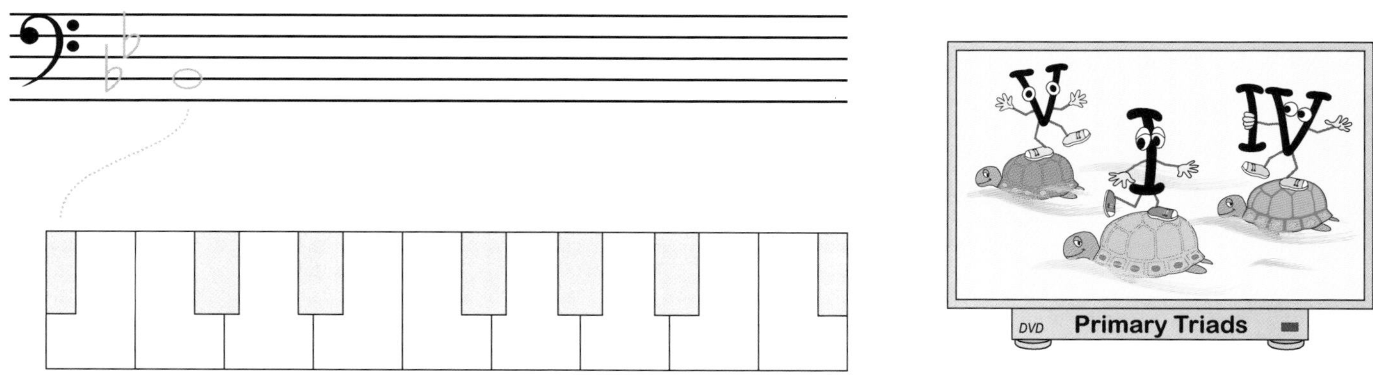

V I IV
DVD Primary Triads

The word adjacent means neighboring. For example, in the alphabet, the letter A is adjacent to B. But A is not adjacent to C. An alternate word for neighboring is a_________________.
Adjacent is pronounced a-JAY-cent. Adjacent means n_______________.

Compare These Scales

Which keys are different?

Name the major scale that you could play on each keyboard, using only the colored keys. Write I, IV, and V on the correct keys. Name each colored black key. Draw lines between the keyboards to show which notes differ across the adjacent scales.

B flat major

B♭ E♭ B♭ E♭

V I IV V I IV

This is E♮, not E♭.

I

IV

I

C♯

IV

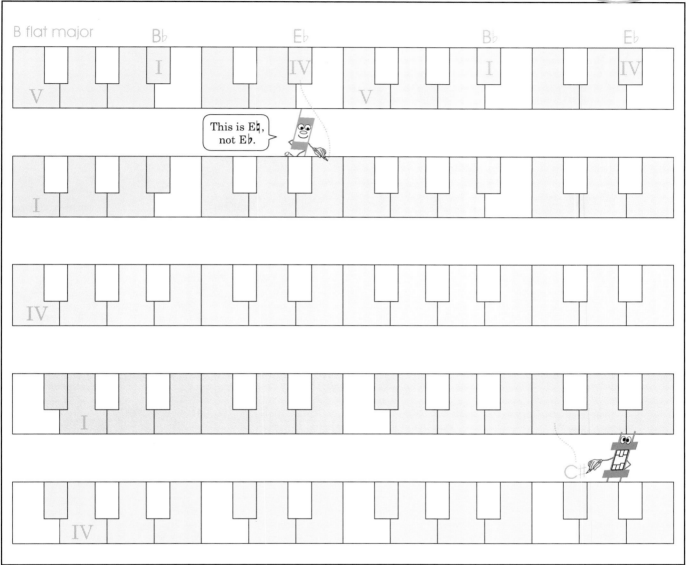

Circle all the scales that each note belongs to. For example, E *natural* can be found in all of the scales listed below it, except B flat major. In contrast, E *flat* belongs to just one of the scales listed.

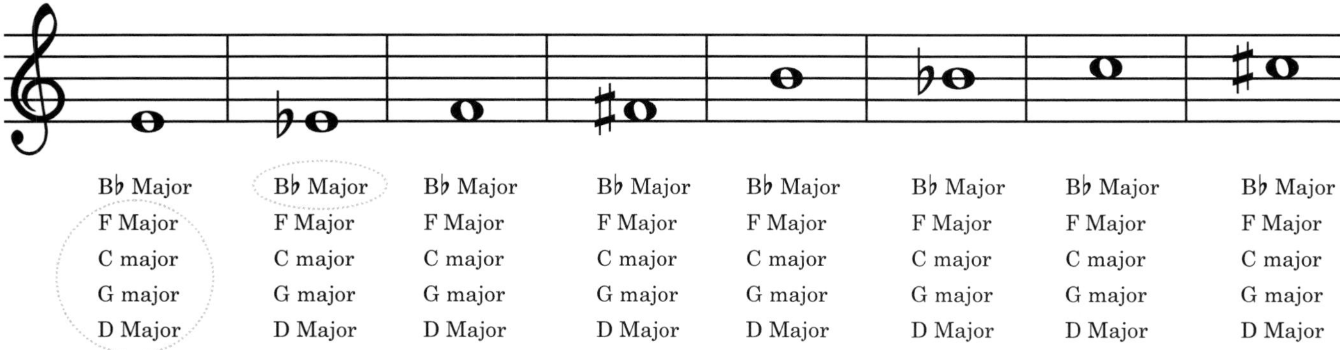
B♭ Major
F Major
C major
G major
D Major

  Published by April Avenue Music. www.DoctorMozart.com 800 567-8878

How to Remember Key Signatures

Trace and name these key signatures. Then write each key signature on your own.

_____ major
_____ major
_____ major
_____ major
Battle Ends
F♯
FATHER CHARLES

The flats in B flat major are _____ and _____. Remember them with the phrase ***Battle Ends.***
The sharps in D major are _____ and _____. Remember them with the phrase ***Father Charles.***

Draw lines to match each phrase with the correct key signature.

Battle Ends **Father Charles**

The sharps and flats in each key signature are always written in the same order.

You can remember the B flat major key signature with two words: ________________ __________
You can remember the D major key signature with two words: ________________ ________________

Below, look at the gray keys on each keyboard. Then at right, write the matching key signatures in the treble staff and bass staff. Name the gray keys.

  Published by April Avenue Music. www.DoctorMozart.com 800 567-8878

What is a Key?

The word *key* has two musical meanings: →

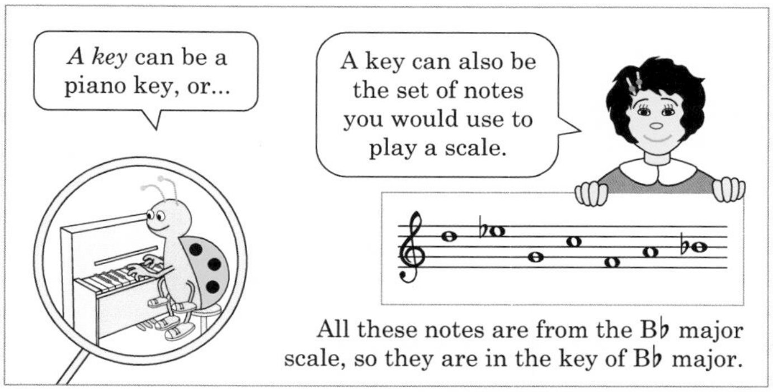

A *key* can be a piano key, or...

A key can also be the set of notes you would use to play a scale.

All these notes are from the B♭ major scale, so they are in the key of B♭ major.

Name these intervals. Then on the right side of each staff, write the key signature that matches the accidentals. Name the key. Write the primary triads.

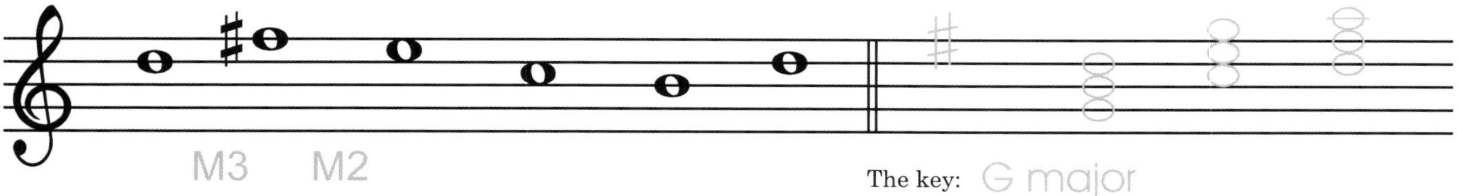

M3 M2

The key: G major

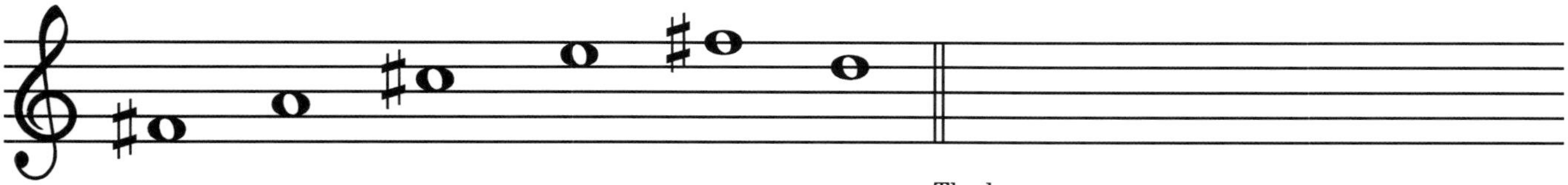

The key:

The key:

The key:

Write the correct clef for each key signature. Name each key signature. Circle each note that should be played with a black key. Name the intervals.

Key Signatures at Work

B flat major

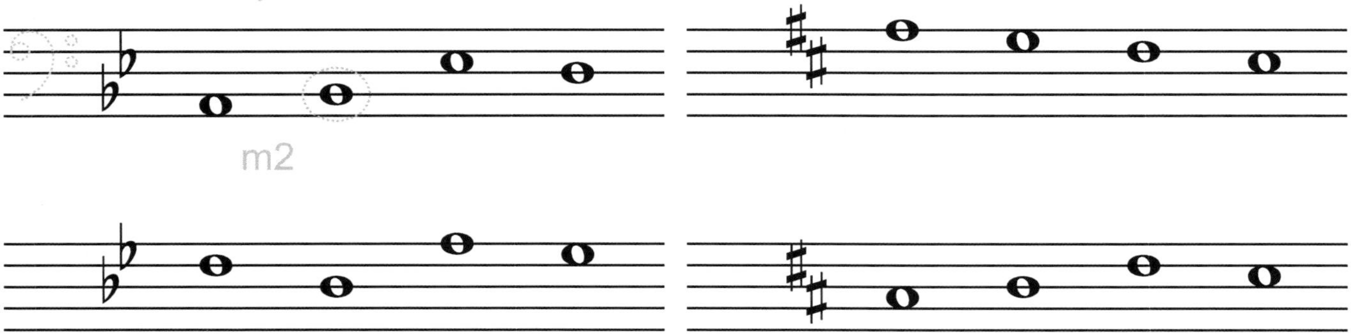

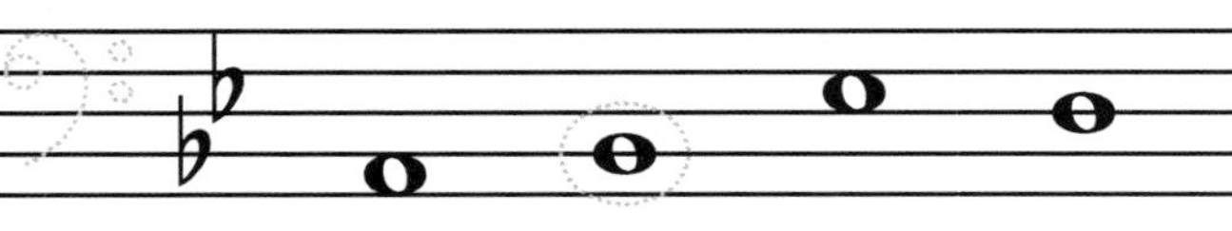

m2

  Published by April Avenue Music. www.DoctorMozart.com 800 567-8878

Triad Test

R

3

5

Write R, 3, and 5 to show the root, 3rd, and 5th of each triad.

I in B flat major

R 3

I in D major

IV in B flat major

R

IV in D major

V in B flat major

V in D major

Write the correct clef for each key signature. Then name the key signatures.

F Major

Dominant

Subdominant

Tonic

Write the correct clef for each key signature. Then write a triad for each Roman numeral.

V IV I

V IV I

V IV I

V IV I

  Published by April Avenue Music. www.DoctorMozart.com 800 567-8878

Black & White 3rds

Write a harmonic interval above each note as indicated. Draw lines to the keyboard.

m3
m3
M3
M3

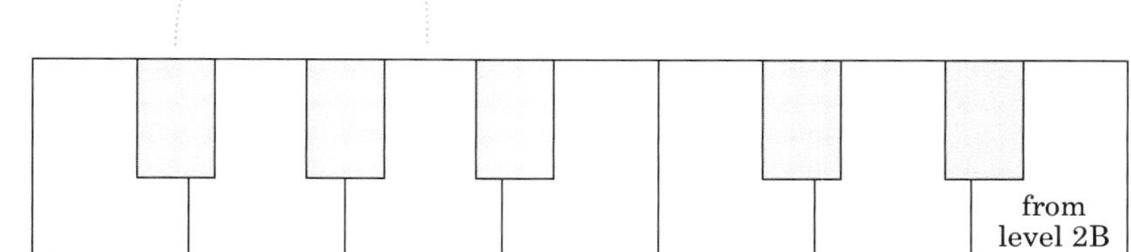
from
level 2B

Write a harmonic interval **below** each note as indicated. Draw lines.

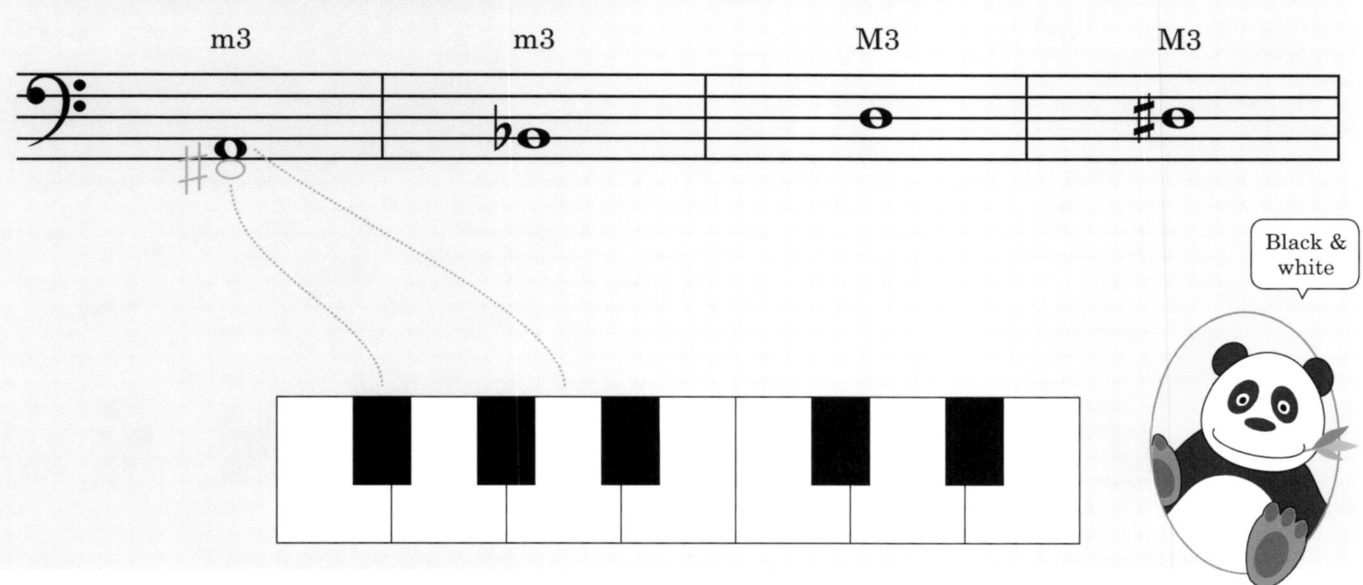
m3
m3
M3
M3
Black & white

Below, write any accidentals needed to make each interval a P5. Then write a major 3rd above each bottom note to form a major triad. Use the keyboard to help find the intervals.

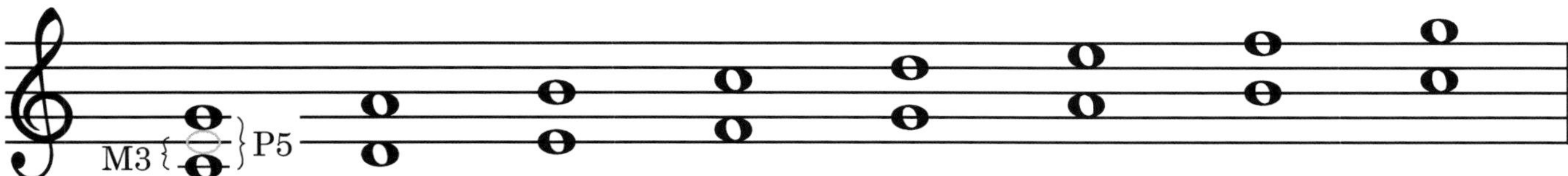
M3
P5

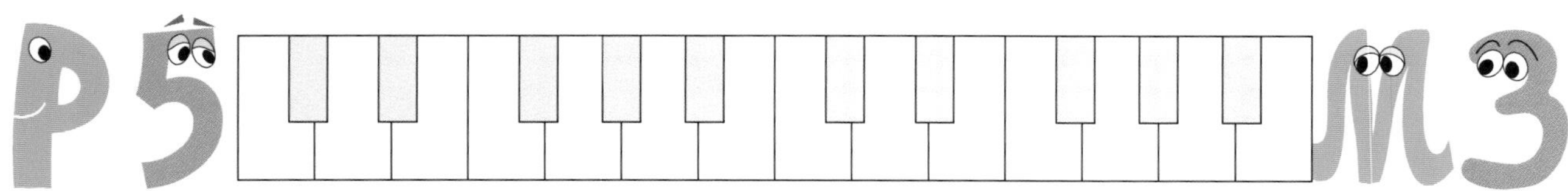
P5
M3

  Published by April Avenue Music. www.DoctorMozart.com 800 567-8878

Black & White 4ths & 5ths

Zebra intervals have one black key and one white key.

Every P4 contains 2½ steps. You can count them in any order. On this staff, write a P4 above each given note. Draw lines. Circle the zebra intervals.

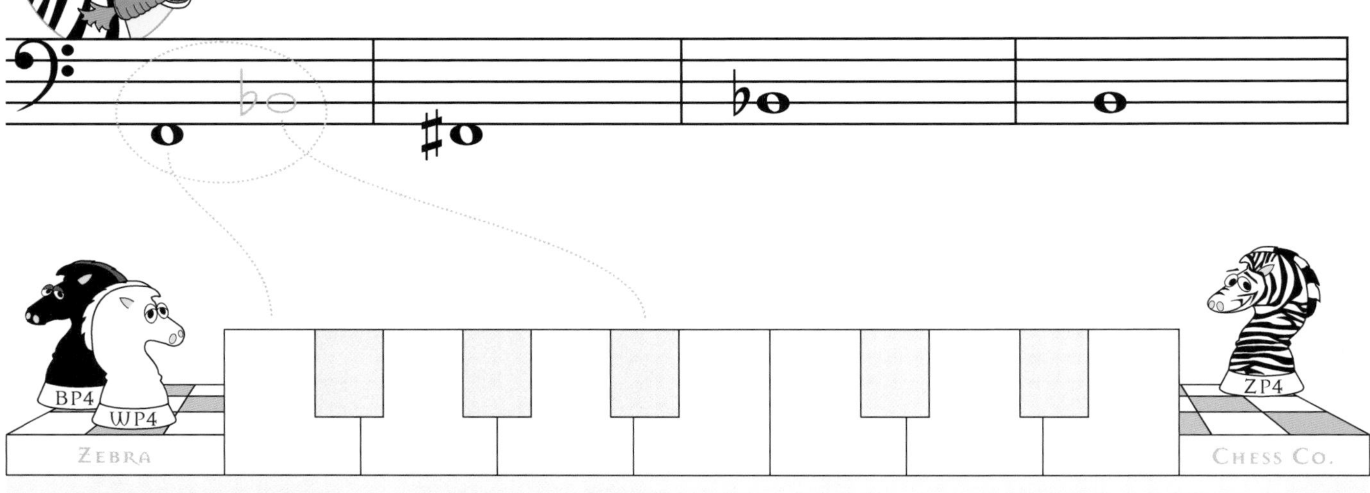
BP4
WP4
ZP4
ZEBRA
CHESS CO.

Every P5 contains 3½ steps. You can count them in any order.
Write a P5 above each given note. Draw lines. Circle the zebra P5s.

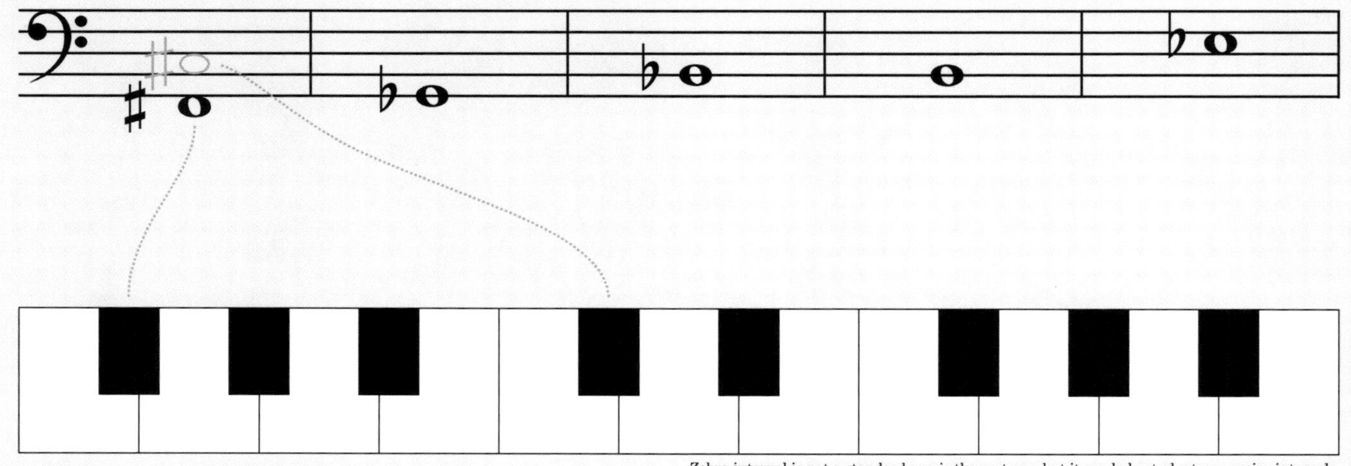

Zebra interval is not a standard music theory term, but it can help students recognize intervals.

Write two different zebra P5s and two different zebra P4s. Draw lines.

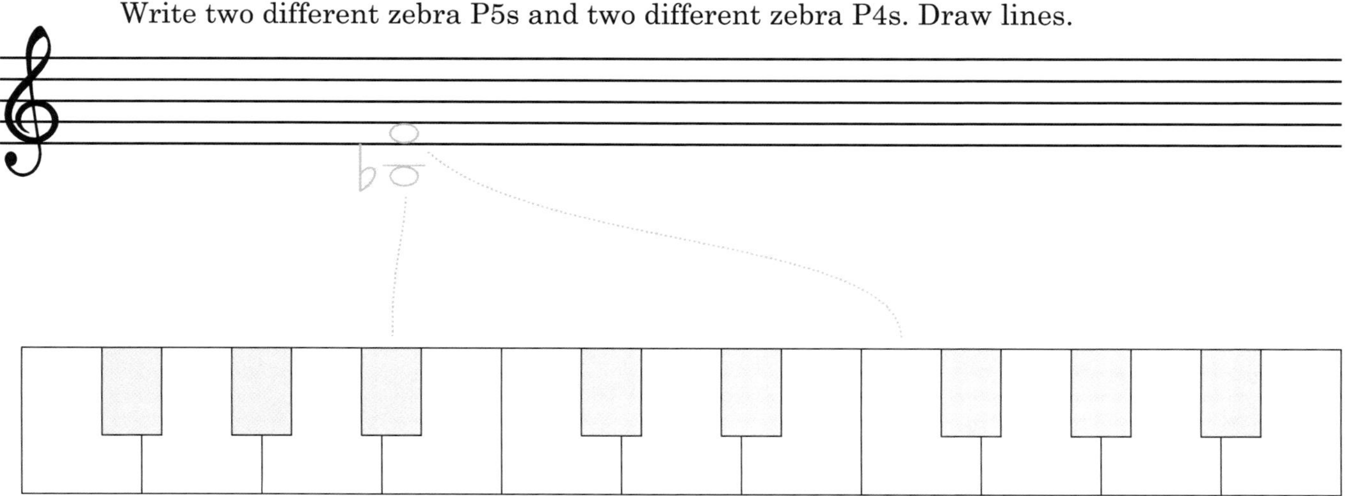

  Published by April Avenue Music. www.DoctorMozart.com 800 567-8878

Natural Minor Scales

Write Roman numerals to complete these two scales. Use only white keys. Draw a V bracket at each semitone. Which scale has a semitone between II and III? ______________________

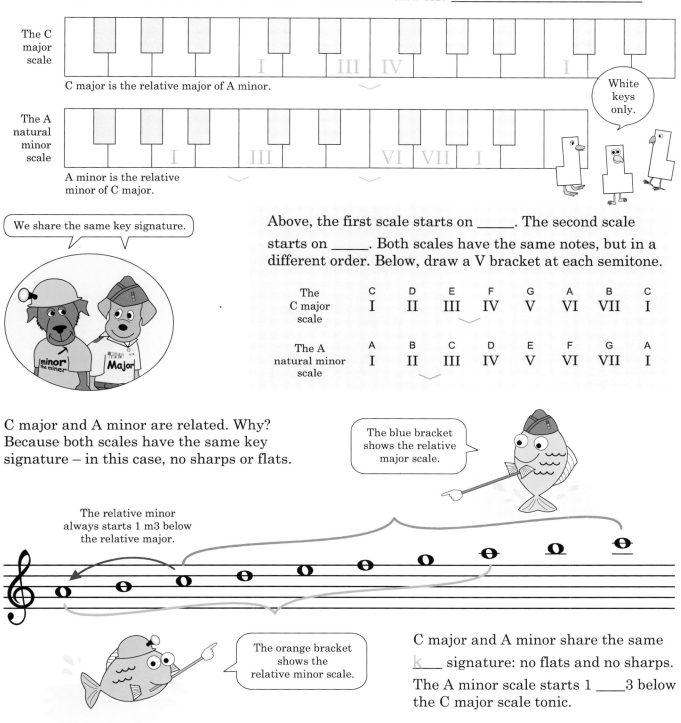

The C major scale: I III IV I

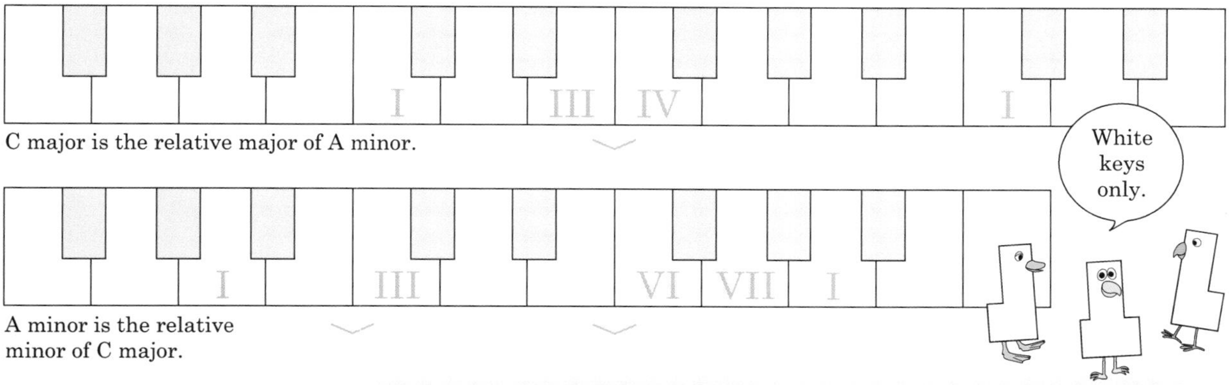

C major is the relative major of A minor.

The A natural minor scale: I III VI VII I

A minor is the relative minor of C major.

White keys only.

We share the same key signature.

minor the miner

Major

Above, the first scale starts on _____. The second scale starts on _____. Both scales have the same notes, but in a different order. Below, draw a V bracket at each semitone.

	C	D	E	F	G	A	B	C
The C major scale	I	II	III	IV	V	VI	VII	I

	A	B	C	D	E	F	G	A
The A natural minor scale	I	II	III	IV	V	VI	VII	I

C major and A minor are related. Why? Because both scales have the same key signature – in this case, no sharps or flats.

The blue bracket shows the relative major scale.

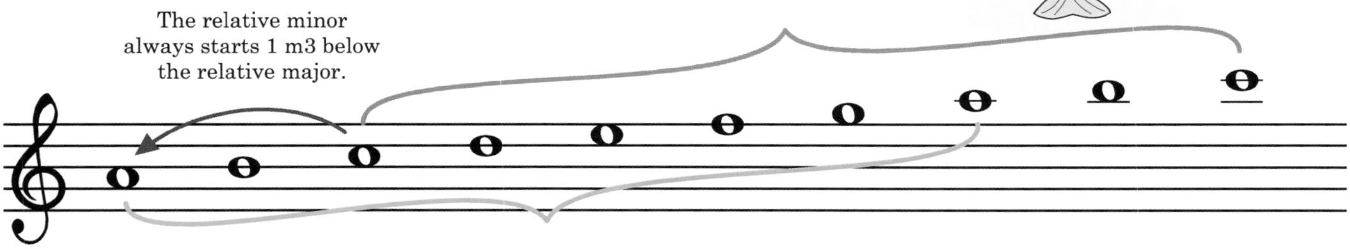

The relative minor always starts 1 m3 below the relative major.

The orange bracket shows the relative minor scale.

C major and A minor share the same k___ signature: no flats and no sharps. The A minor scale starts 1 ___3 below the C major scale tonic.

Next, each named key is the tonic of a major scale. Label the relative minor tonic with a lower case letter. Draw an arrow to connect each pair of tonic notes.

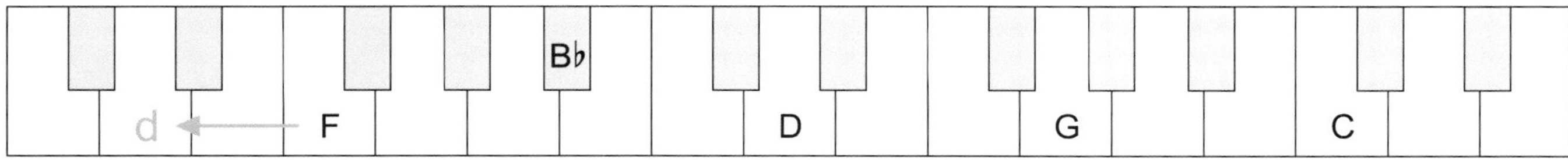
B♭
d
F
D
G
C

  Published by April Avenue Music. www.DoctorMozart.com 800 567-8878

Relative Major & Minor Scale Quiz

Here, each major scale is followed by its relative minor, which has the same key signature.

Name the notes in each scale.
Mark each semitone with a V bracket.

G major

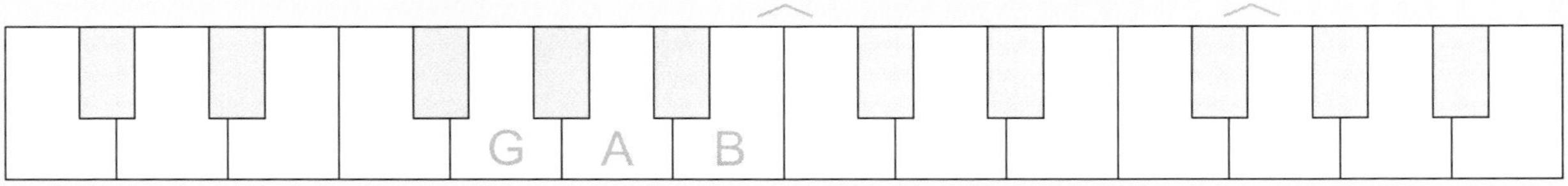

G A B

E natural minor

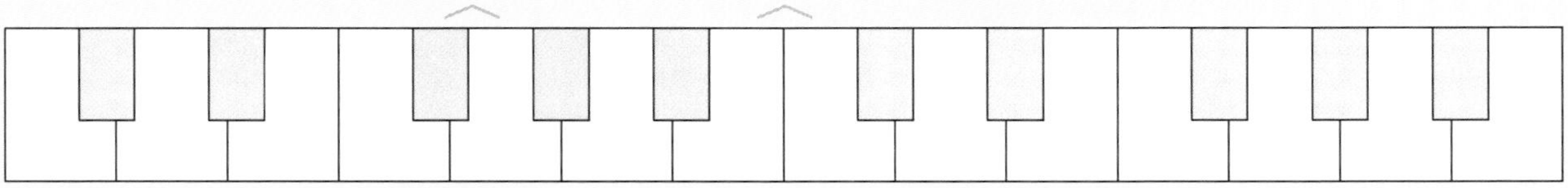

F major

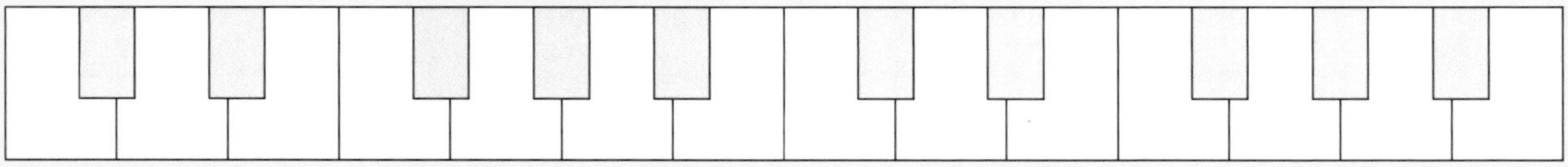

D natural minor

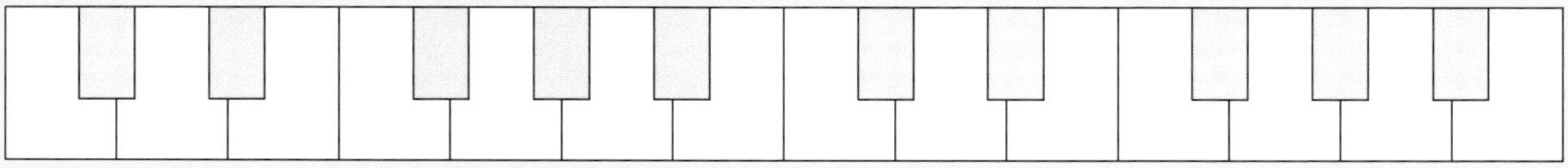

D major

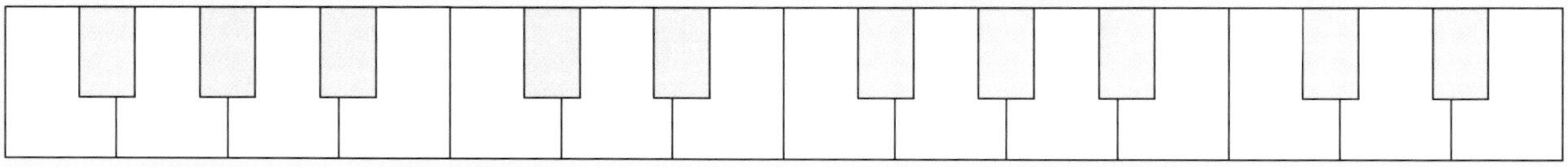

B natural minor

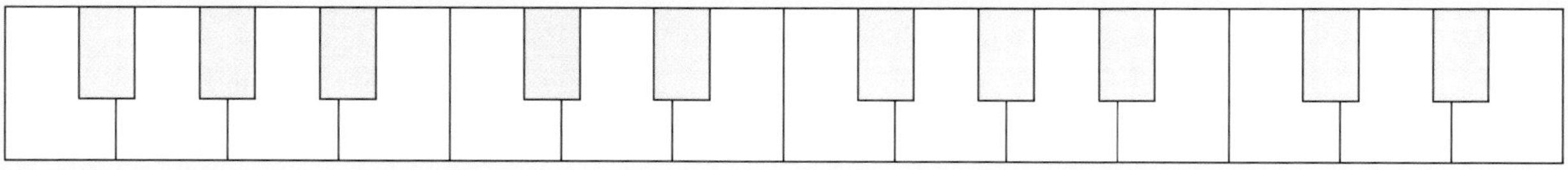

B flat major

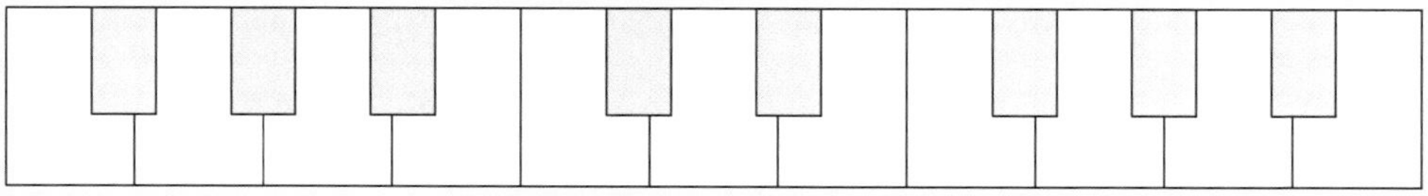

G natural minor

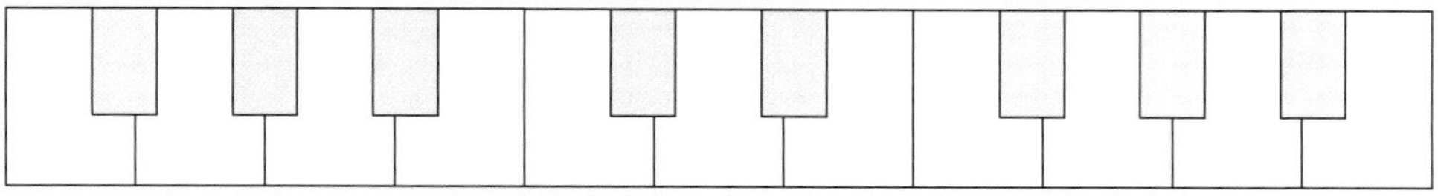

  Published by April Avenue Music. www.DoctorMozart.com 800 567-8878

More Relatives

A
B
C
D
E
F
G
A

Write the correct key signatures.
Write the scales, ascending. Draw lines.

D major

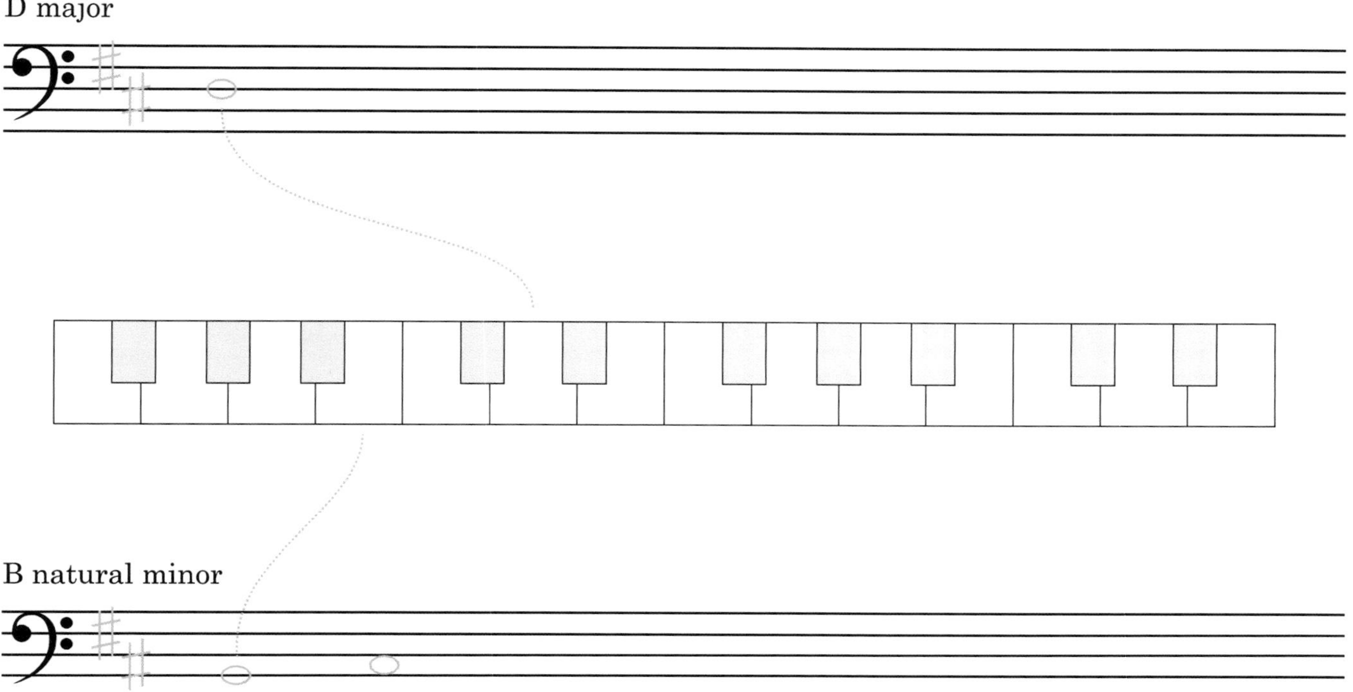

B natural minor

B♭ major

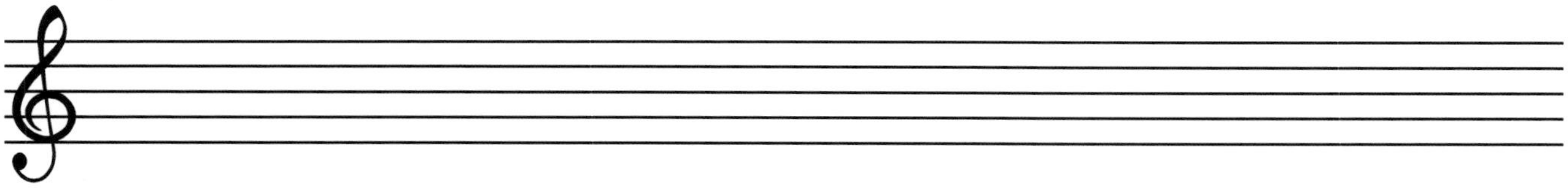

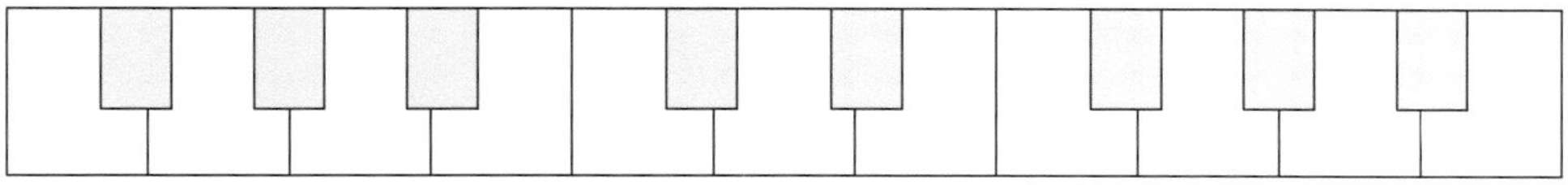

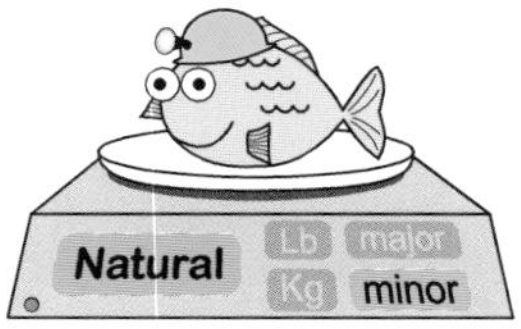

G natural minor

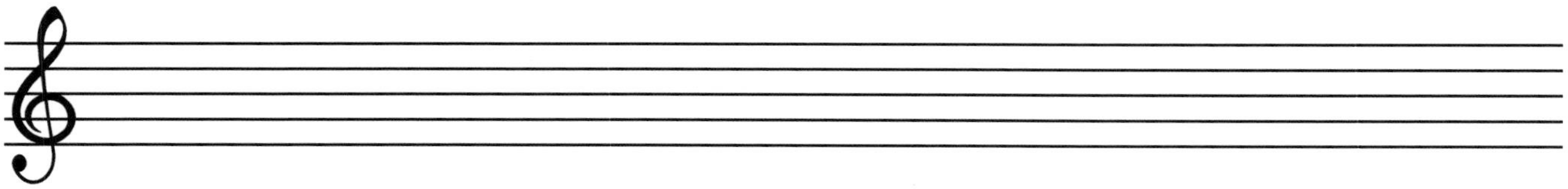

Key Signature Quiz

Battle Ends
Father Charles
Battle Ends
FATHER CHARLES

Draw lines to match each phrase with the correct key signature.

Father Charles	B♭ major
Battle Ends	D major

Write these key signatures. M = major. m = minor.

GM	Em	DM	Bm	B♭M	Gm	FM	Dm

Each printed note is the tonic note of a minor scale. Write the correct key signatures. Name them. Use no more than 2 sharps or 2 flats.

______ minor
______ minor
______ minor
______ minor

Write the correct clefs. Name each key signature two ways: As a major key, and as the relative minor.

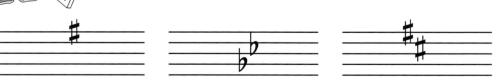

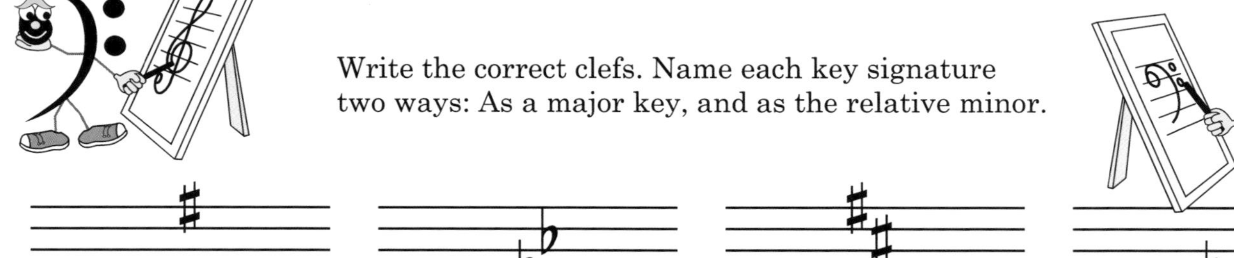

___ major ___ minor ____ major ____ minor ___ major ___ minor ___ major ___ minor

  Published by April Avenue Music. www.DoctorMozart.com 800 567-8878

How to Invert Intervals

Each of these keyboards has an orange paw interval. If you raise the lowest paw note by one octave, you can make the blue paw interval. Name the intervals.

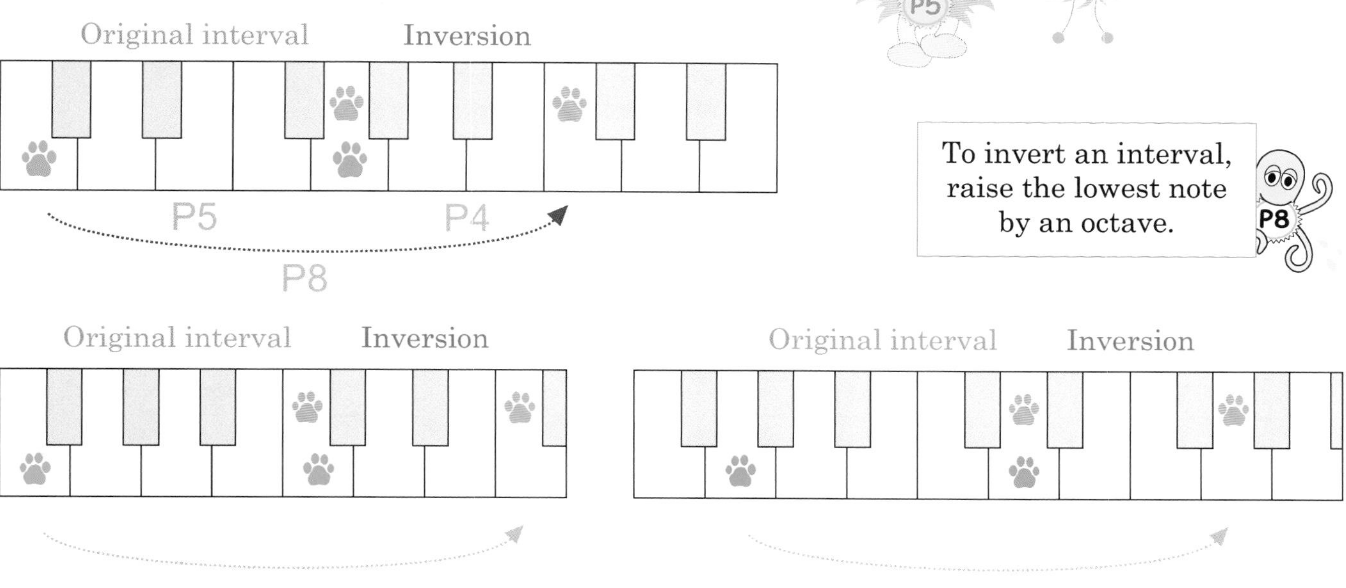
Original interval
Inversion
P5
P4
P8
P4
P5
To invert an interval, raise the lowest note by an octave.
P8
Original interval
Inversion
Original interval
Inversion

To invert an interval, raise the lowest note by an O_______________.

Next, for each paw print interval, let's raise the lowest note by an octave. Label the keys that form each inversion. Name the intervals.

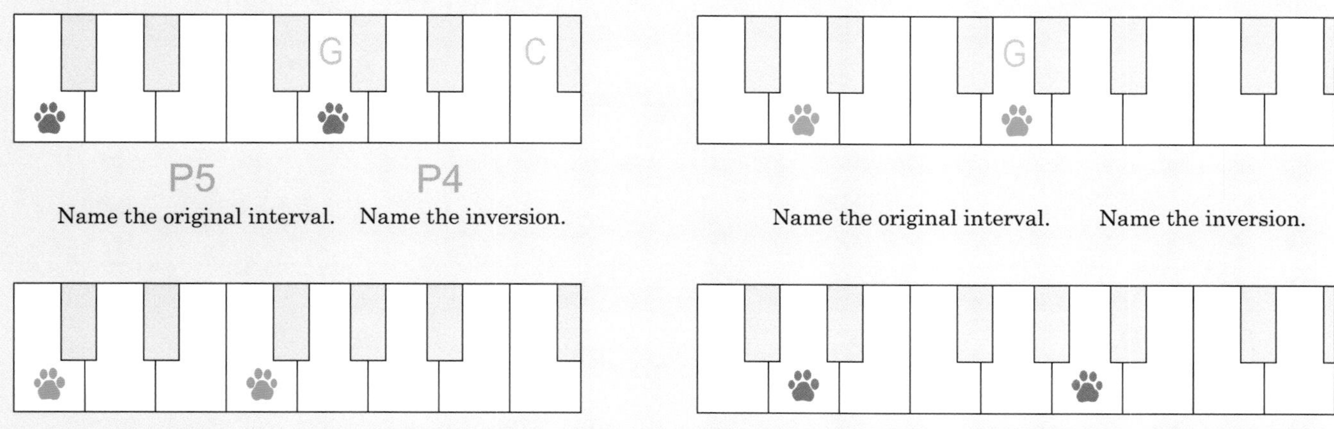
G
C
G
P5
P4
Name the original interval.
Name the inversion.
Name the original interval.
Name the inversion.
P4

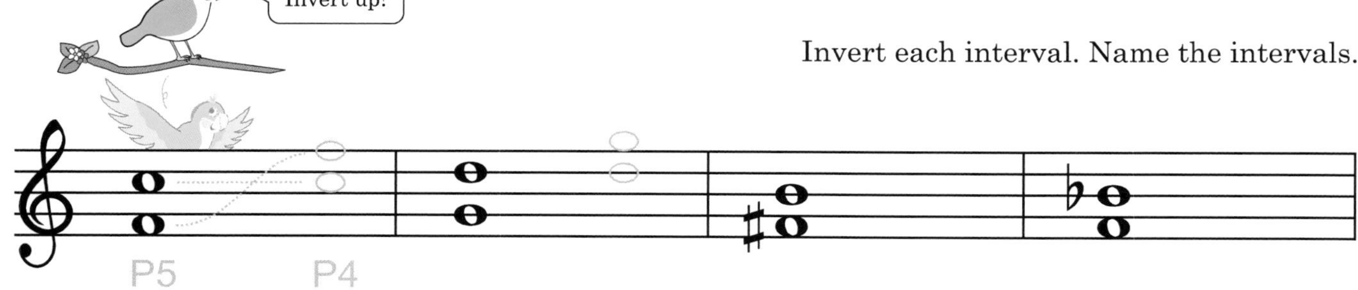
Invert up!
Invert each interval. Name the intervals.
P5
P4

 © MMVIII, MMXIII Machiko and Paul Christopher Musgrave. Published by April Avenue Music. www.DoctorMozart.com 800 567-8878

How to Invert Downward

P5
P4

To invert an interval downward, lower the highest note by a P8.

Lower the highest note by an octave.

Invert each of these paw print intervals downward. Label the keys that form each inversion. Name the intervals.

P8

C F

P4 P5 P4

P8

Invert each interval downward. Name the intervals.

P4 P5

Below, draw lines to connect the green Zs. Name the intervals.
Draw lines to connect the red Zs. Name the intervals.

Zebra 4ths and 5ths.

P4 P5

P5

  Published by April Avenue Music. www.DoctorMozart.com 800 567-8878

Which is Bigger: P5 or M6?

Write the note names in the boxes. Use neighboring letters. Draw brackets.

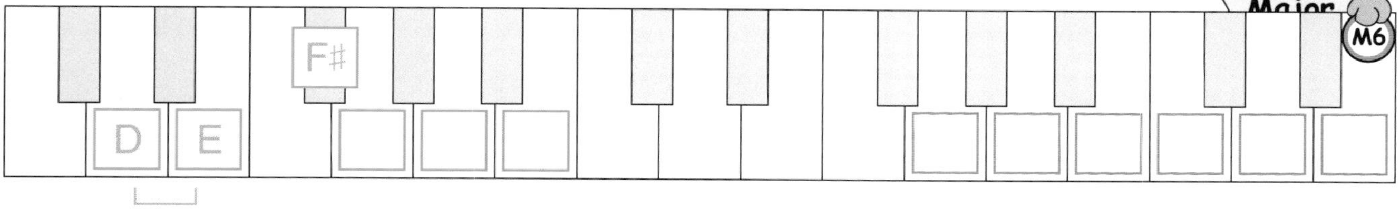

Major M6

F♯ D E

Each group makes a major 6th (M6). An M6 is one W__________ step wider than a P5.

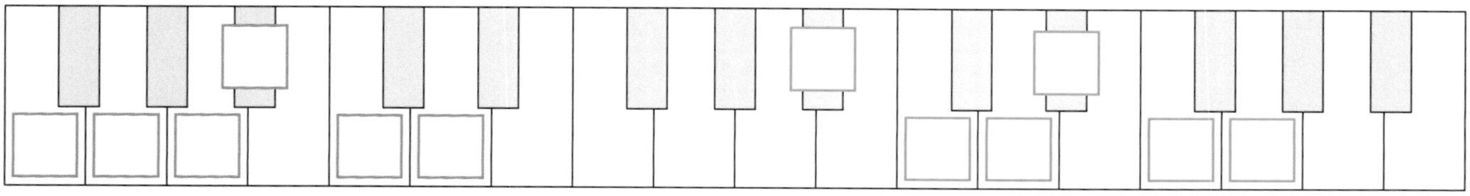

M6 = major 6th.

A major 6th is one whole step larger than a perfect 5th.

M6 P5 M6

One whole step larger.

Below, name the keys that form a P5 and M6 above each named key.

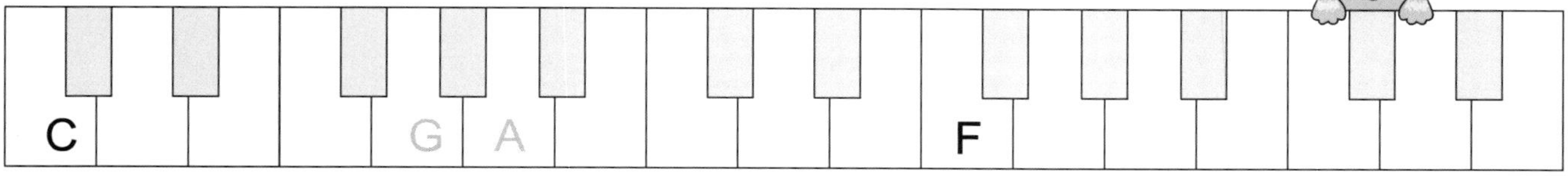

C G A F

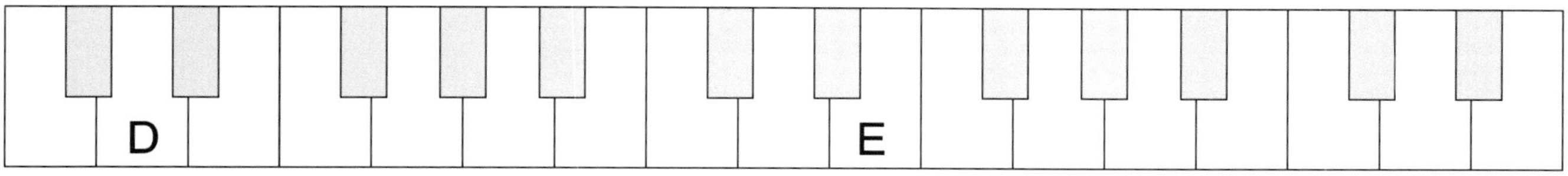

D E

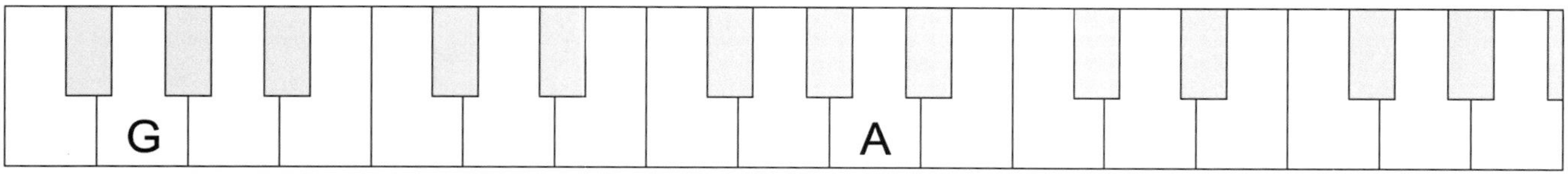

G A

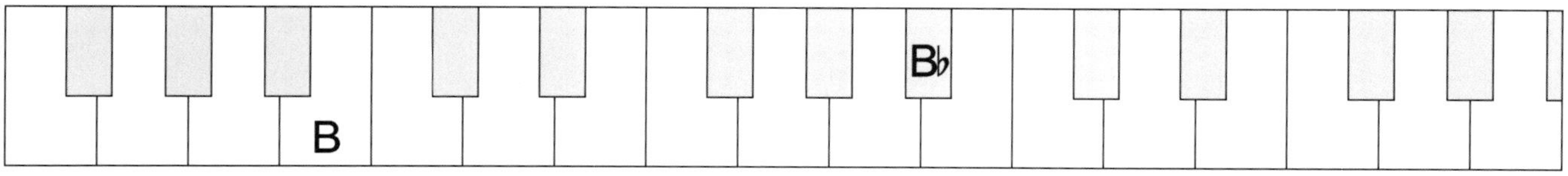

B B♭

  Published by April Avenue Music. www.DoctorMozart.com 800 567-8878

A Smaller 6th

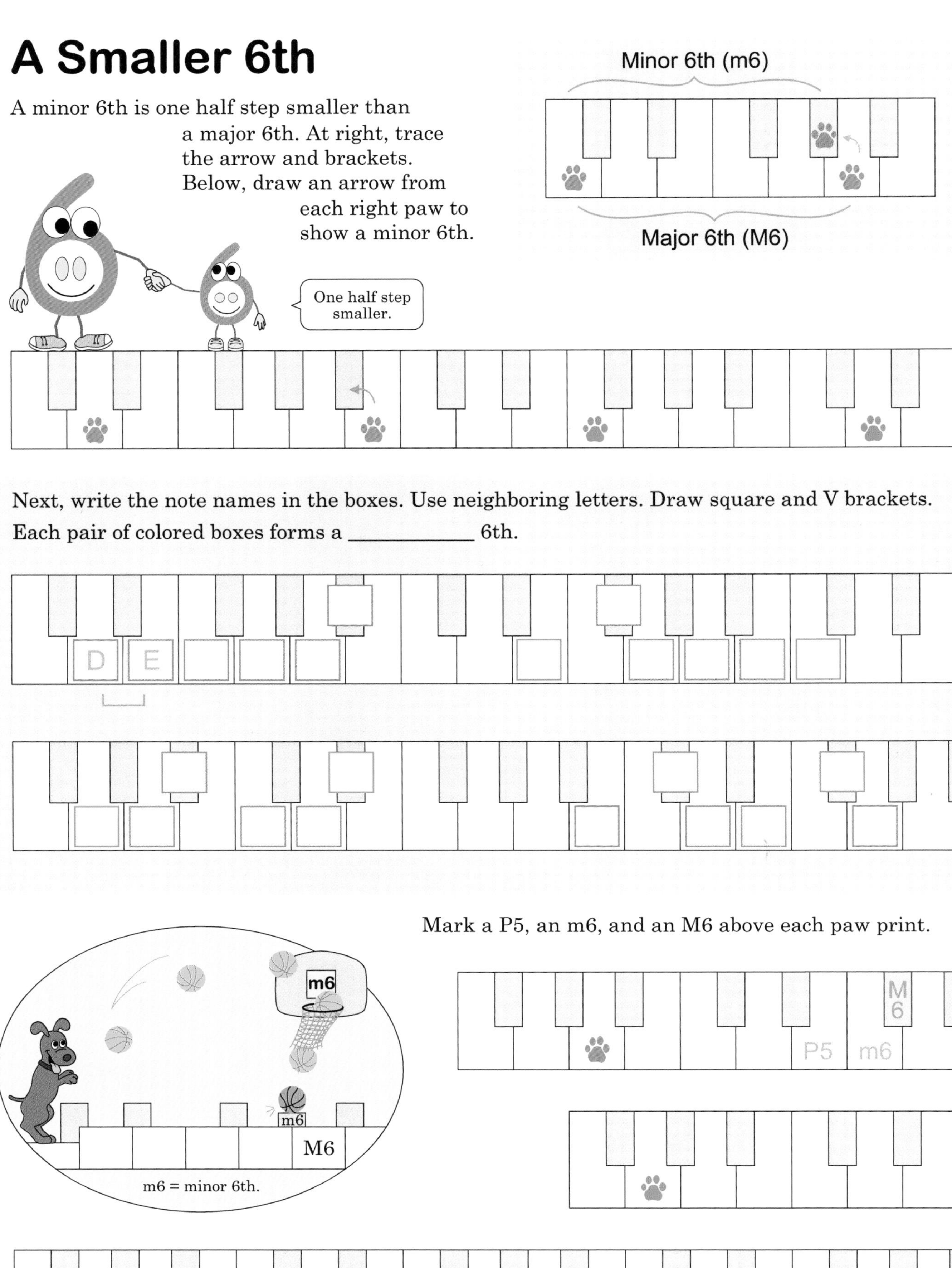
Minor 6th (m6)
Major 6th (M6)
One half step smaller.
D
E
M
6
P5
m6
m6
m6
M6
m6 = minor 6th.

A minor 6th is one half step smaller than a major 6th. At right, trace the arrow and brackets. Below, draw an arrow from each right paw to show a minor 6th.

Next, write the note names in the boxes. Use neighboring letters. Draw square and V brackets. Each pair of colored boxes forms a ___________ 6th.

Mark a P5, an m6, and an M6 above each paw print.

  Published by April Avenue Music. www.DoctorMozart.com 800 567-8878

An M7 is Almost an Octave

Write the note names in the boxes. Use neighboring letters. Draw brackets. Trace the arrows. Each pair of colored boxes forms a major 7th.

M7

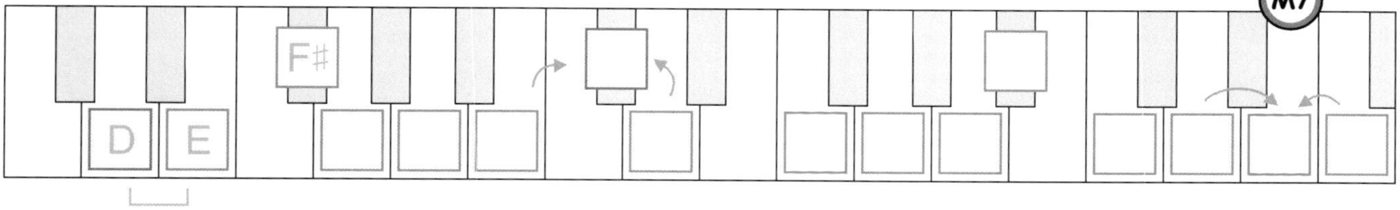

F♯

D E

The arrows show that a major 7th is one w________ step larger than a major 6th, and one h________ step smaller than a perfect octave.

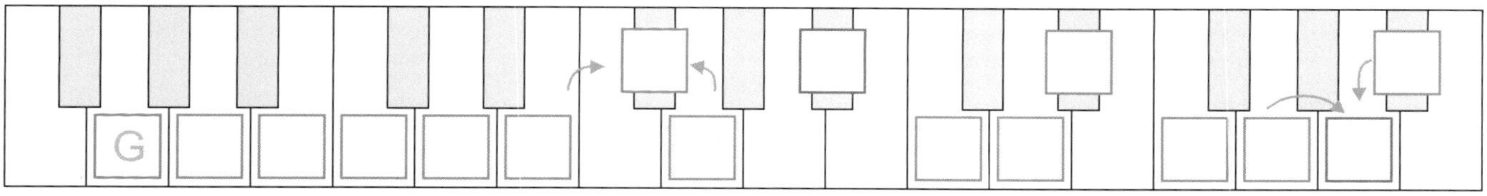

G

Below, name the notes that are a P8 and an M7 above each named key.

M7 P8

A major 7th is 1 half step smaller than an octave.

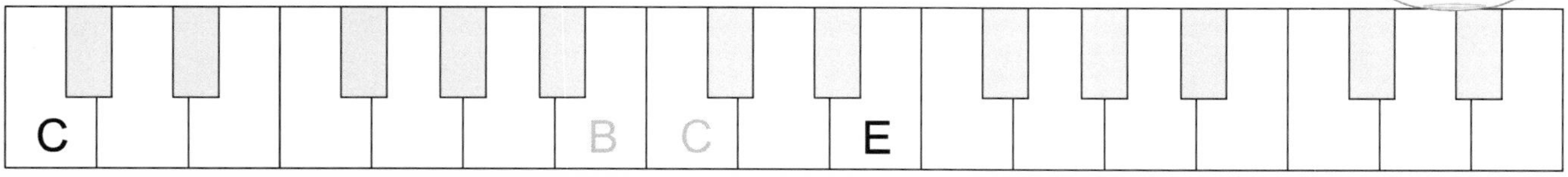

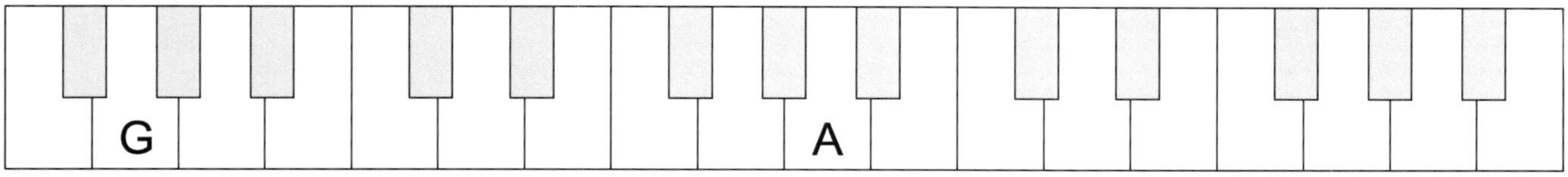

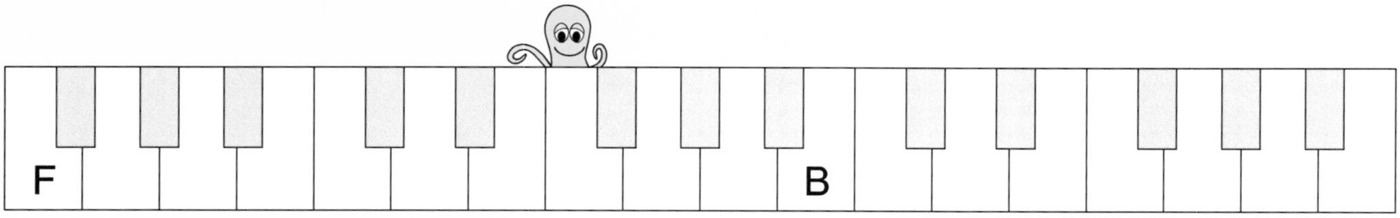

C B C E

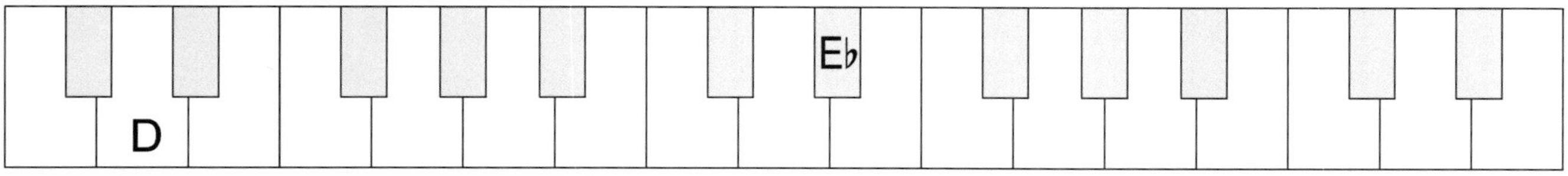

D E♭

G A

F B

  Published by April Avenue Music. www.DoctorMozart.com 800 567-8878

A Smaller 7th

A minor 7th
is one half step
smaller than
a major 7th.

Below, trace the brackets and the arrow.

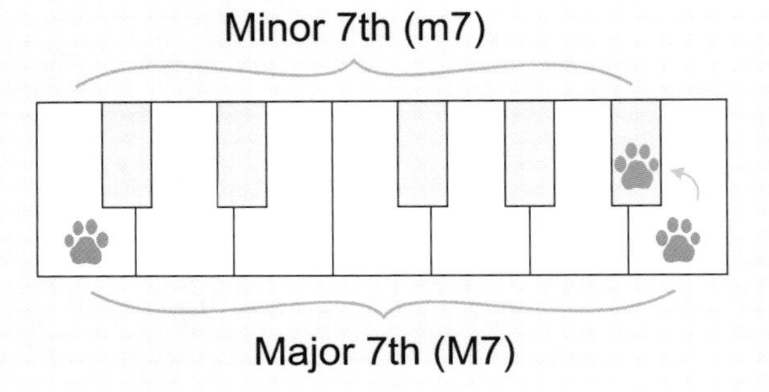
Minor 7th (m7)
Major 7th (M7)

Below, draw an arrow from each right paw print to show a minor 7th.

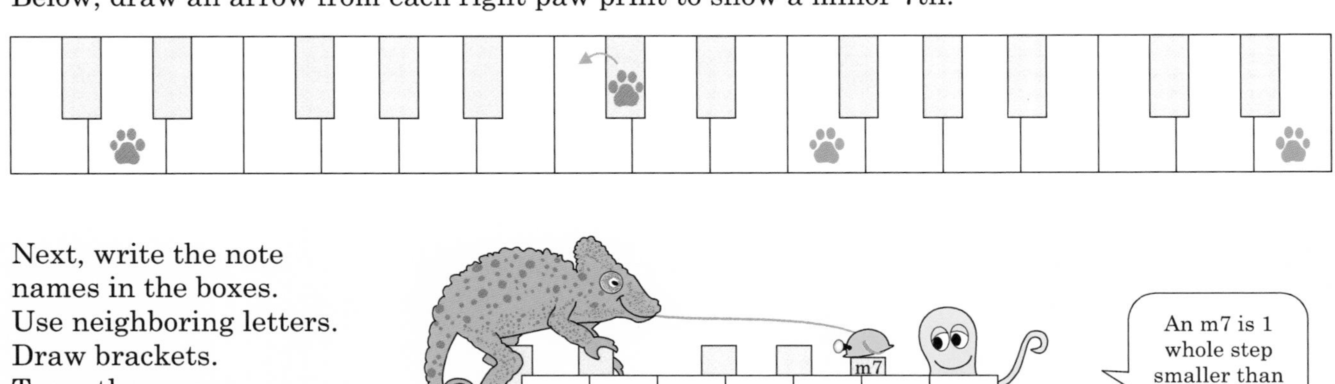

Next, write the note names in the boxes.
Use neighboring letters.
Draw brackets.
Trace the arrows.

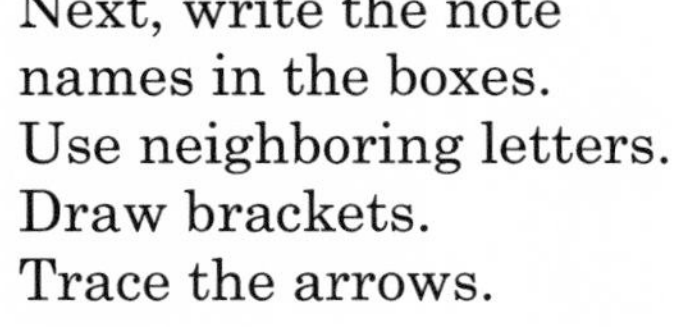
m7
P8
An m7 is 1
whole step
smaller than
an octave.

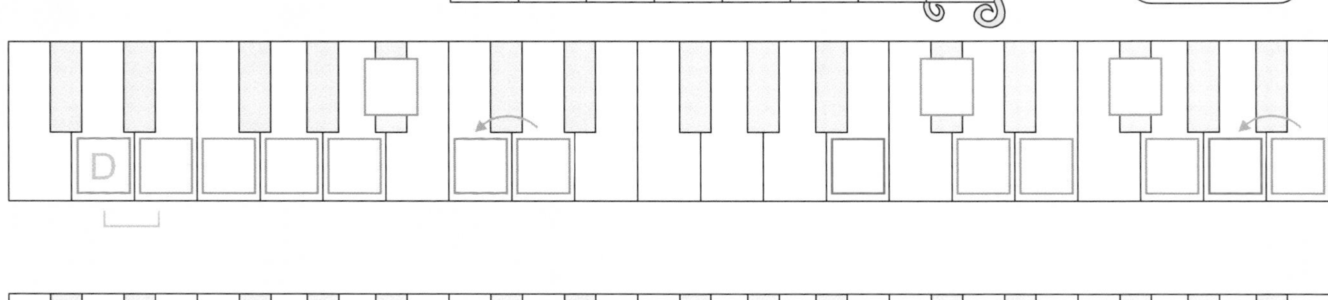
D

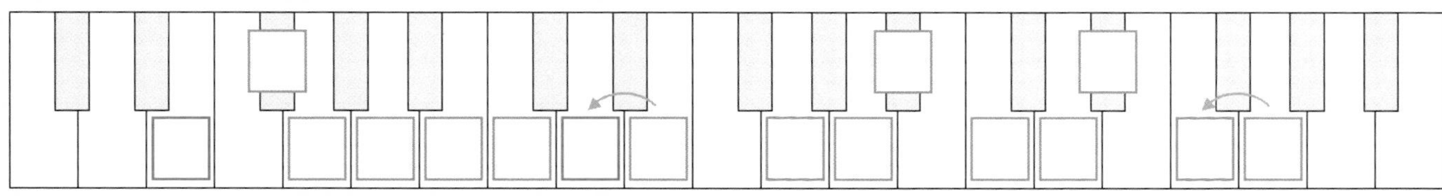

Mark a P8, an M7, and an m7 above each paw print.

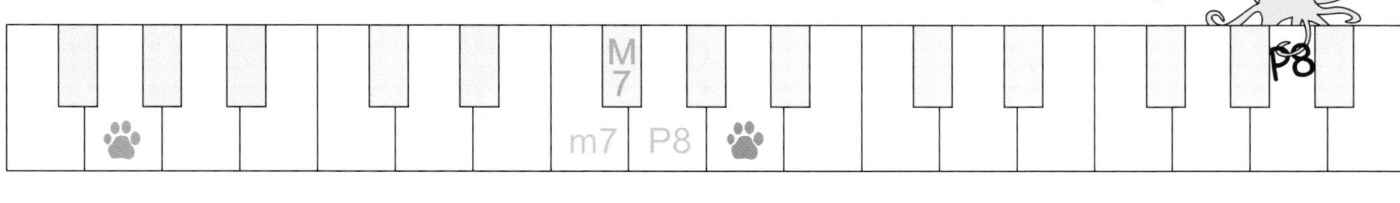
M
7
m7
P8
P8

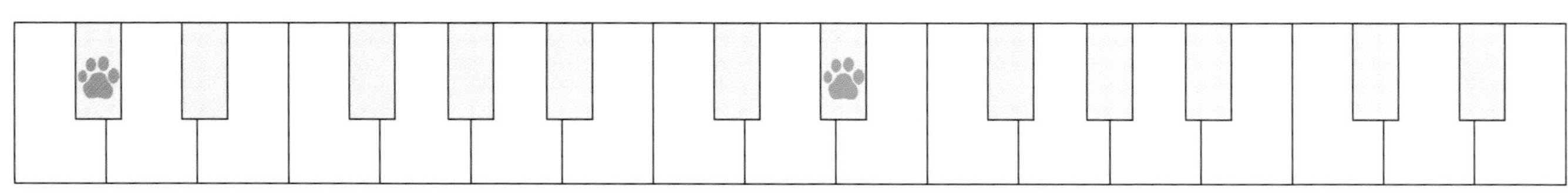

How to Add Intervals

As you know, we add numbers like this: 2 + 2 = 4. But intervals are different. They add up in surprising ways, like this: M2 + M2 = M3. Or m2 + m2 = M2. Below, write an equation for each pair of intervals.

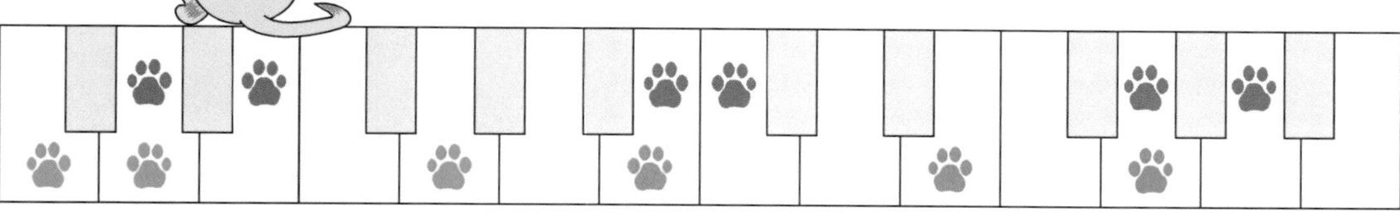

M2 + M2 = M3 M3 + m2 = P4

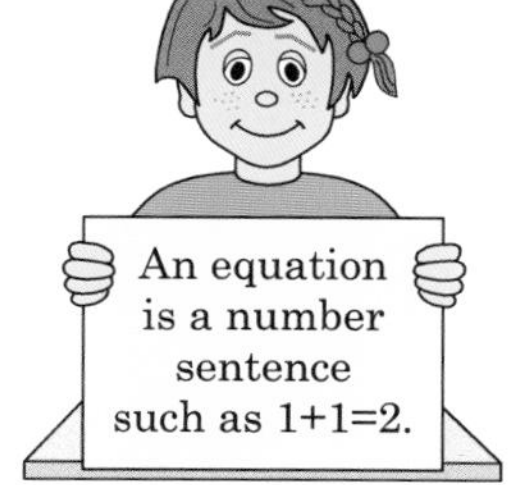
An equation is a number sentence such as 1+1=2.

Before you add two intervals, be sure that the top note of one interval is the bottom note of the other.

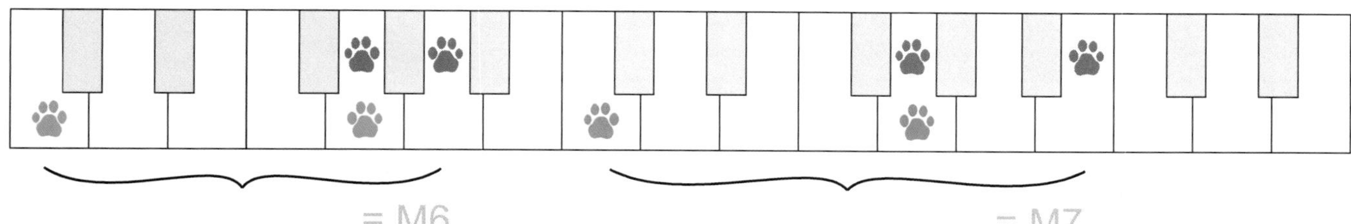

= M6 = M7

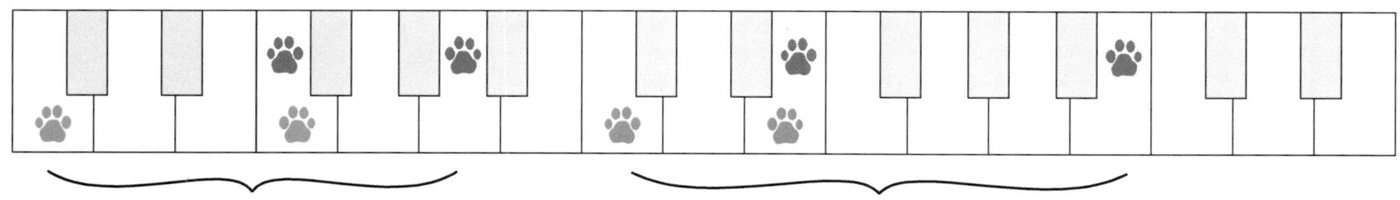

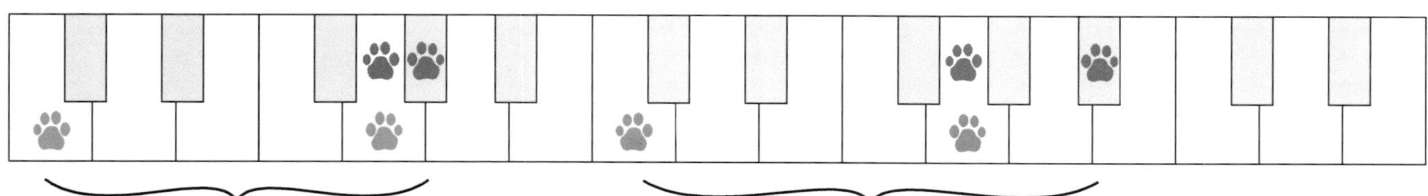

Under this keyboard, write an equation for each paw print triad.

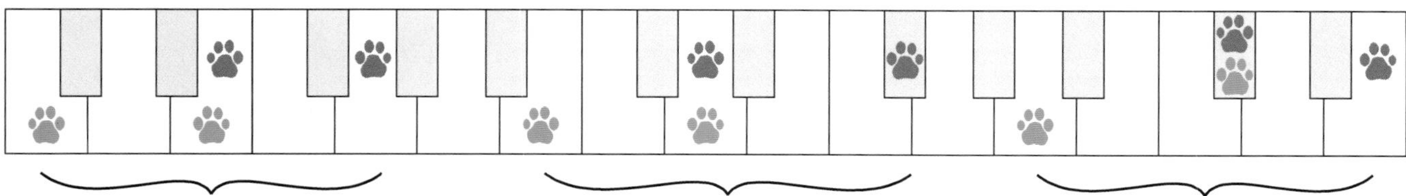

Now you know that M3 + m3 = P_____. Also, m3 + M3 = P_____.

More Inversions

Write an equation for this pair of intervals.

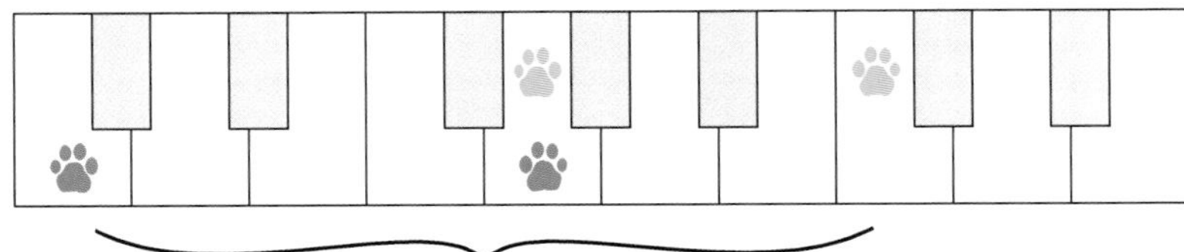

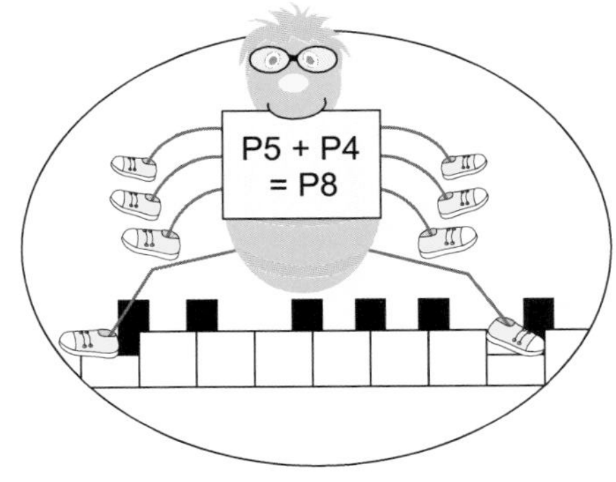
P5 + P4
= P8

Do the above two intervals above add up to a P8? ________.

An interval and its inversion always add up to one octave. Write equations for these intervals:

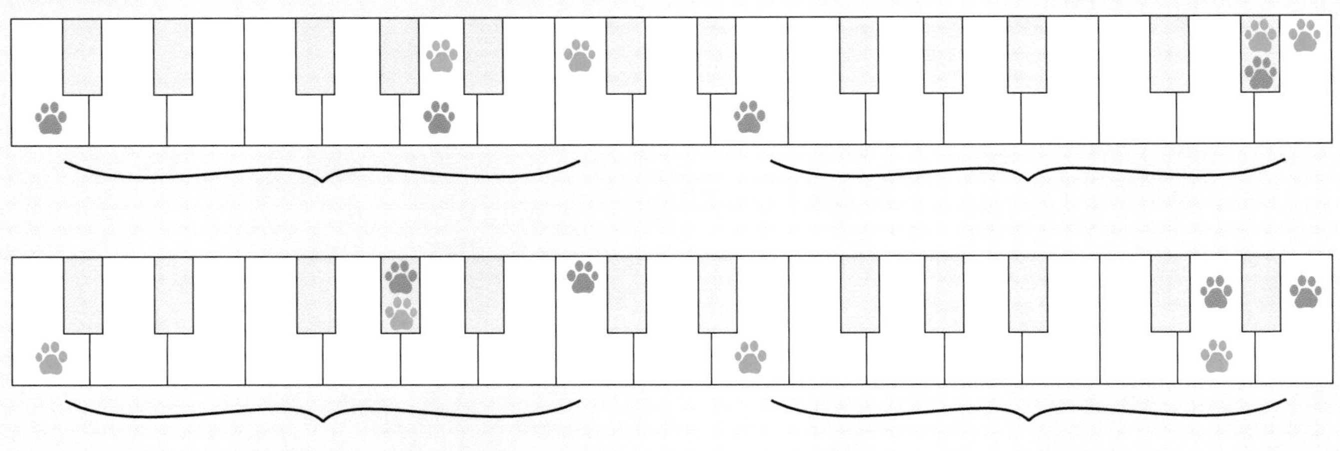

The inversion of a *major* interval is always *minor*. The inversion of a *perfect* interval is always *perfect*. Complete these equations:

M6 + ____3 = P8 M3 + ____6 = P8 m2 + ____7 = P8

m6 + ____3 = P8 M7 + ____2 = P8 m7 + ____2 = P8

m3 + ____6 = P8 P5 + ____4 = P8 P4 + ____5 = P8

Interval	Inversion
Major →	Minor
Minor →	Major
Perfect →	Perfect

An interval and its inversion are known as complementary intervals.

For each paw print interval, label the notes that form the inversion. Write the equations.

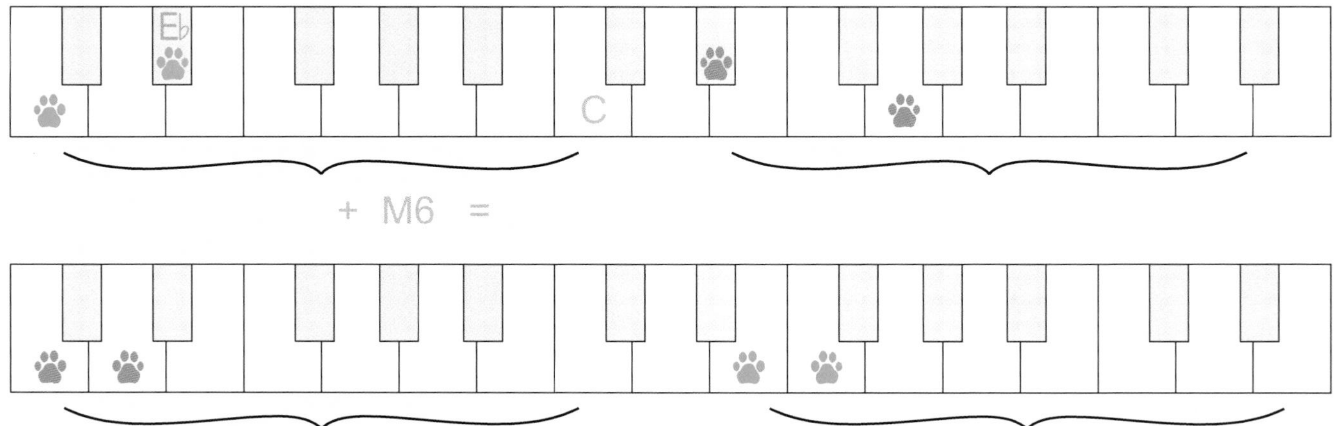
E♭
C
+ M6 =

  Published by April Avenue Music. www.DoctorMozart.com 800 567-8878

Odd and Even Intervals

Some intervals are named with even numbers, such as m2, P4, M6, or P8. The rest are named with odd numbers, such as P1, M3, P5, or m7. Circle the even intervals:

odd
1,3
5,7

m2	P5	P4	m3	m6
P8	P1	m7	M2	M3

2,4
even
6,8

Name these intervals. Circle the even intervals.

m3

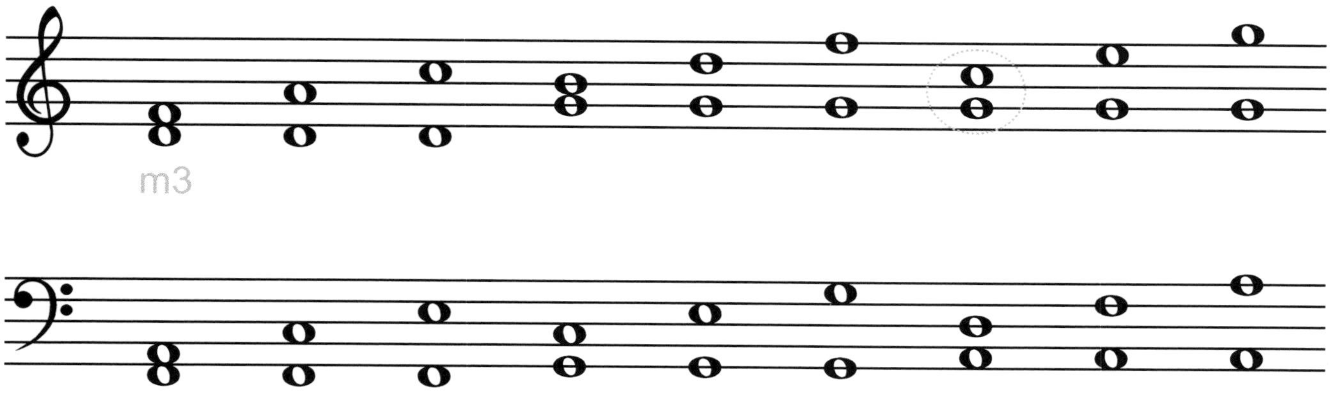

Next, write some intervals that contain accidentals.
Name the intervals. Circle the even intervals.

Odd

Even

On each staff below, make all the intervals either major or perfect by writing the correct clef and key signature (G major or F major). Name the intervals. Circle the even intervals.

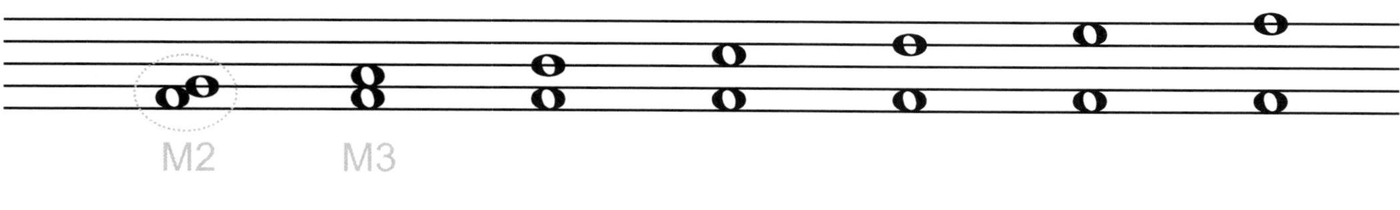
M2
M3

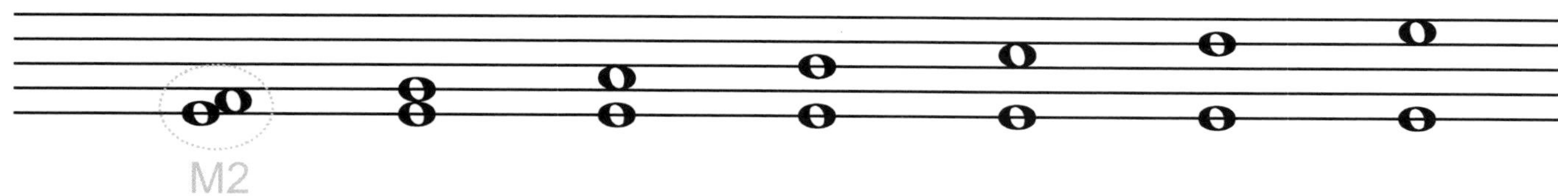
M2

  Published by April Avenue Music. www.DoctorMozart.com 800 567-8878

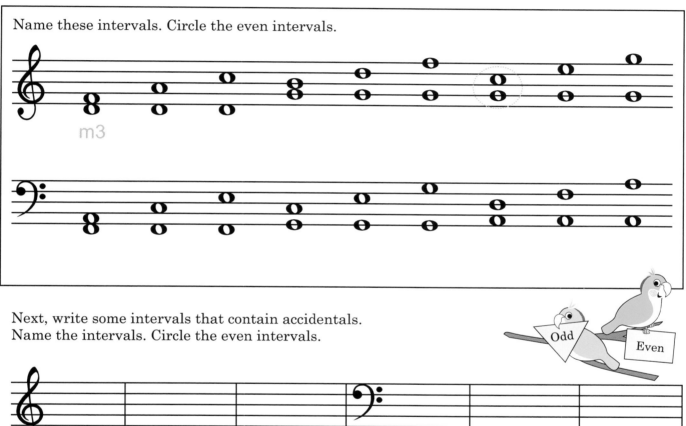

6th & 7th Practice

Label the keys that are a P5, m6, M6, m7, M7, and P8 above each colored key.

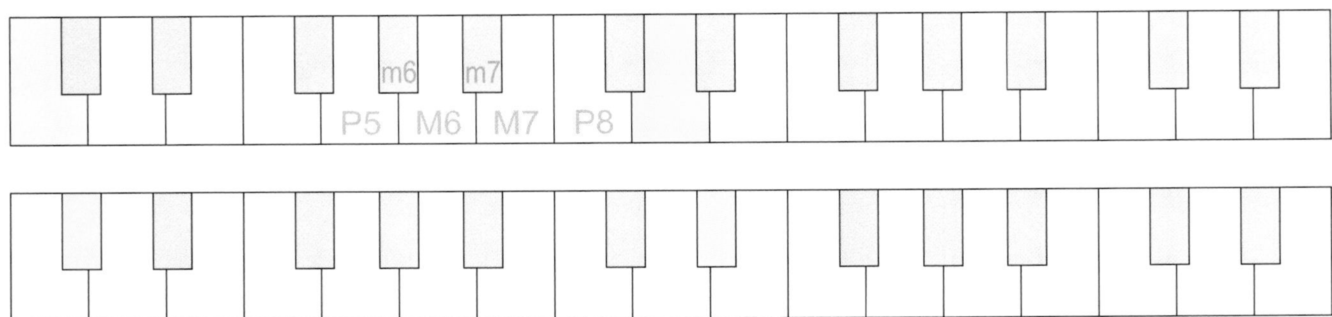
m6
m7
P5
M6
M7
P8

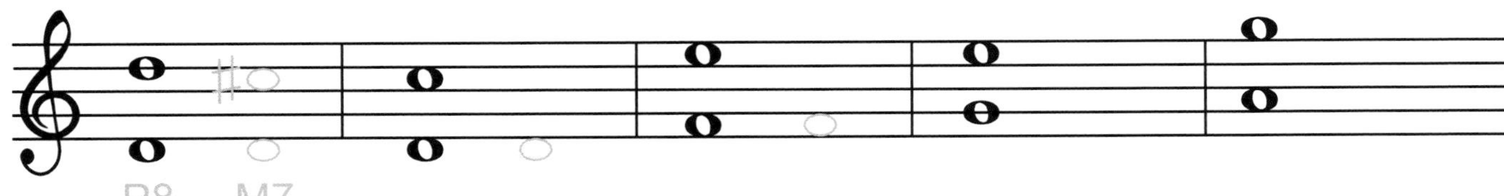

After each given interval, write an interval that has the same bottom note, but is a half step *smaller*. Be sure that the new interval is perfect, major, or minor. Name all the intervals.

P8 M7

After each given interval, write an interval that has the same bottom note, but is a half step *larger*. Be sure that the new interval is perfect, major, or minor. Name all the intervals.

M6 m7

In each bar, write a 6th or 7th, followed by an interval that is one semitone larger. Name the intervals.

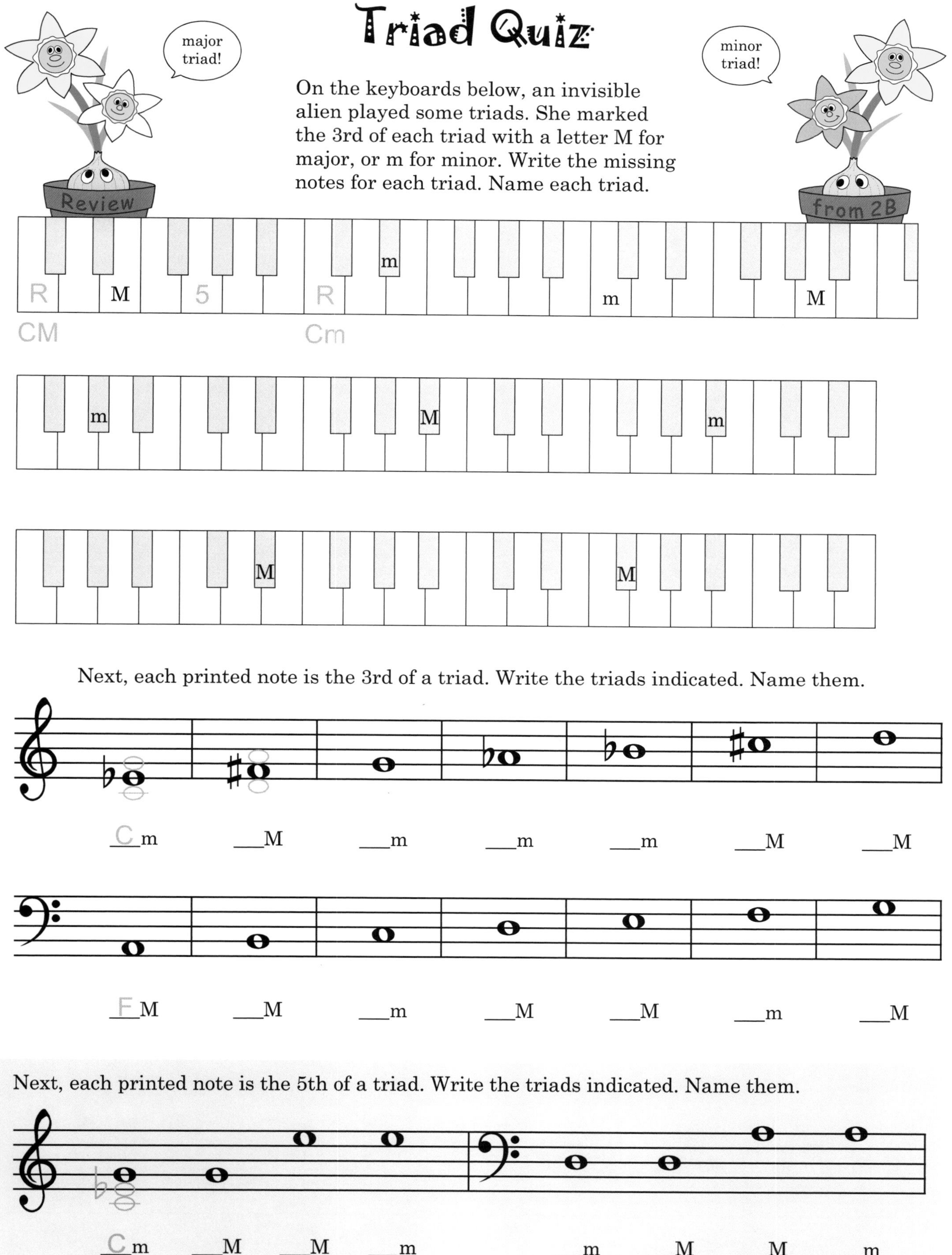
Triad Quiz
major triad!
minor triad!
On the keyboards below, an invisible alien played some triads. She marked the 3rd of each triad with a letter M for major, or m for minor. Write the missing notes for each triad. Name each triad.
Review
from 2B
R M 5 R m m M
CM Cm
m M m
M M
Next, each printed note is the 3rd of a triad. Write the triads indicated. Name them.
C m ___M ___m ___m ___m ___M ___M
F M ___M ___m ___M ___M ___m ___M
Next, each printed note is the 5th of a triad. Write the triads indicated. Name them.
C m ___M ___M ___m ___m ___M ___M ___m

Harmonic Minor Scales

In harmonic minor scales, always write an accidental such as ♯ or ♮ to raise the leading note.
minor the miner

The A *natural* minor scale has no accidentals.

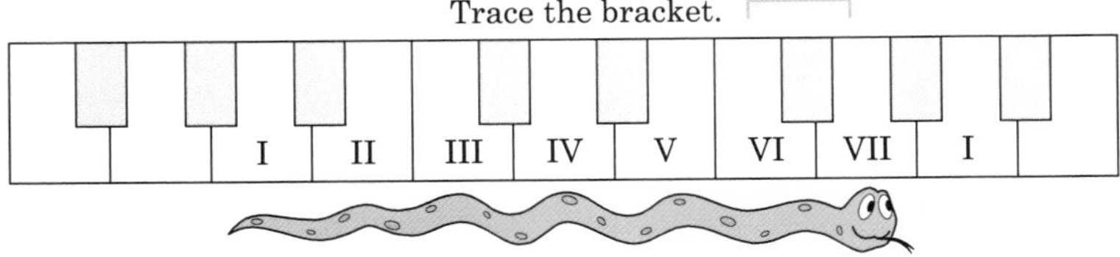
Trace the bracket.
I
II
III
IV
V
VI
VII
I

The A ***harmonic*** minor scale has a raised leading note.

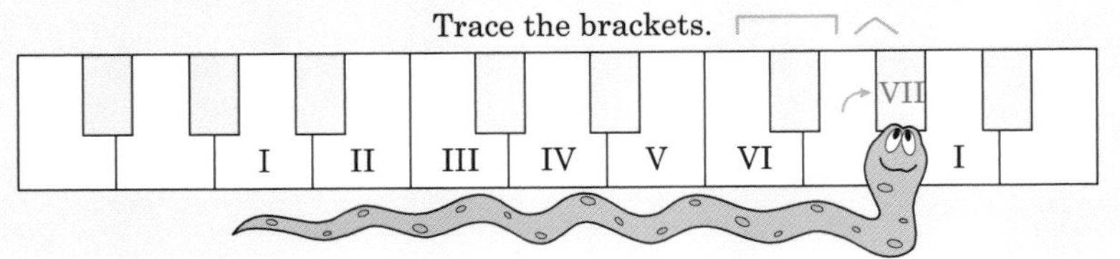
Trace the brackets.
I
II
III
IV
V
VI
VII
I

Since the 7th note is raised, it is more than a whole step away from the 6th note of the scale. That's why there are *two* brackets – a square *and* a V – between those notes.

Next, write the key signatures and ascending scales indicated. Draw lines.

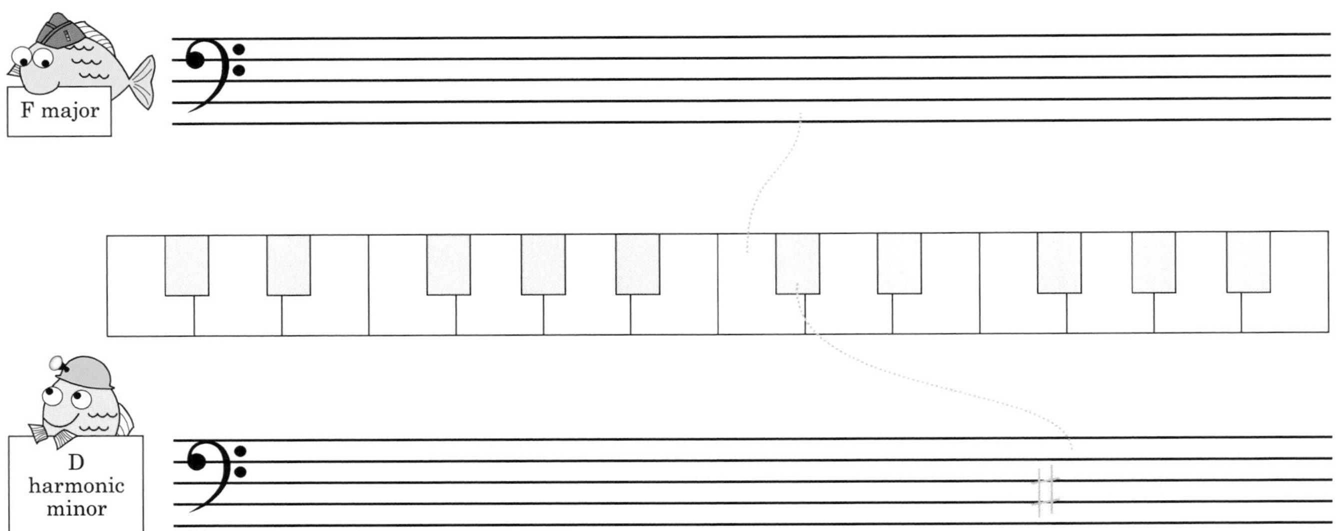
F major
D harmonic minor

Convert each natural minor scale to a harmonic minor scale by raising the leading note. Draw square and V brackets.

Test Your Relatives

We share
the same
key signature.

On each staff, write the key signature and ascending scale. Draw square and V brackets. Draw lines to the keyboard.

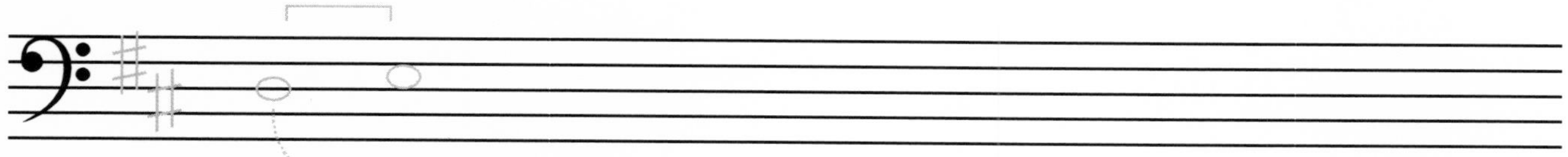

D major

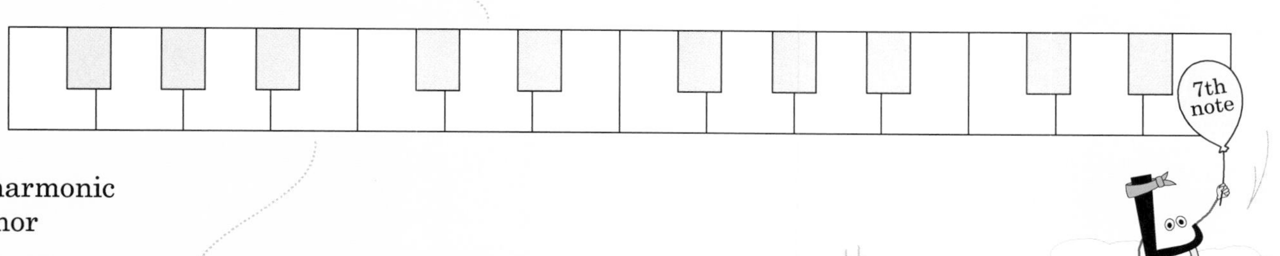

B harmonic minor

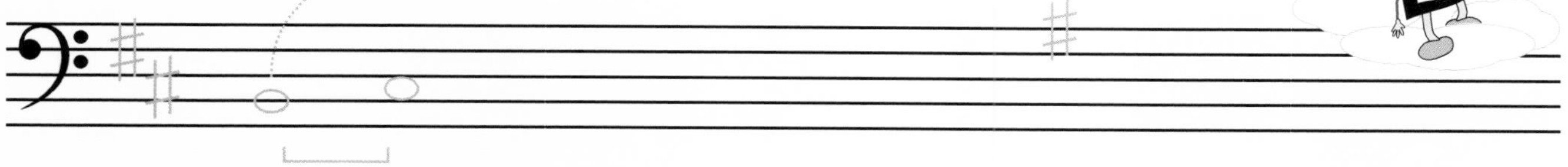

7th note

B♭ major

In harmonic minor scales, always raise the 7th note.

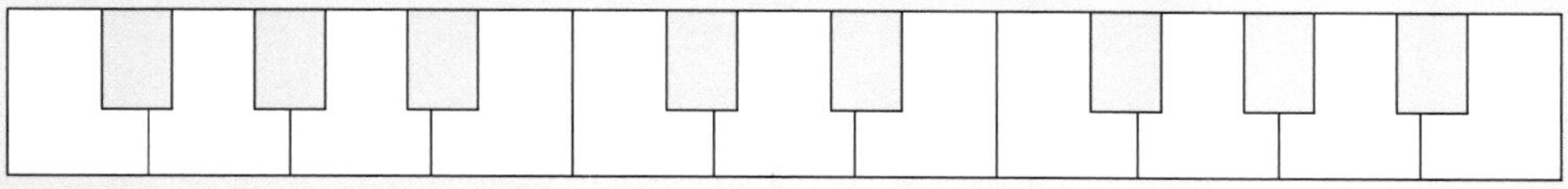

G harmonic minor

Write the correct clefs. Name each key signature two ways: As a major key, and as its relative minor.

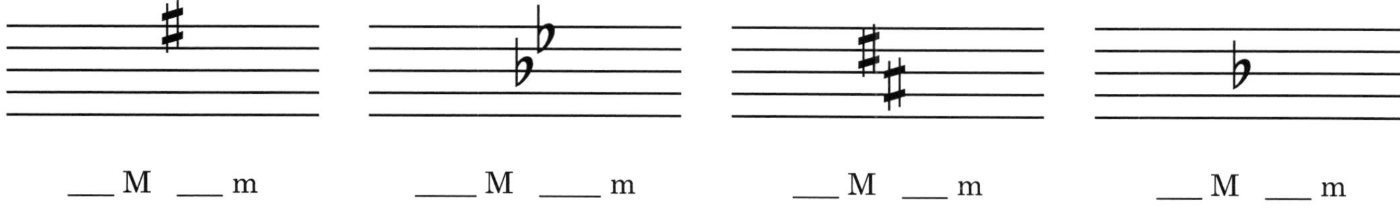
___ M ___ m
___ M ___ m
___ M ___ m
___ M ___ m

  Published by April Avenue Music. www.DoctorMozart.com 800 567-8878

Primary Triads in Harmonic Minor Scales

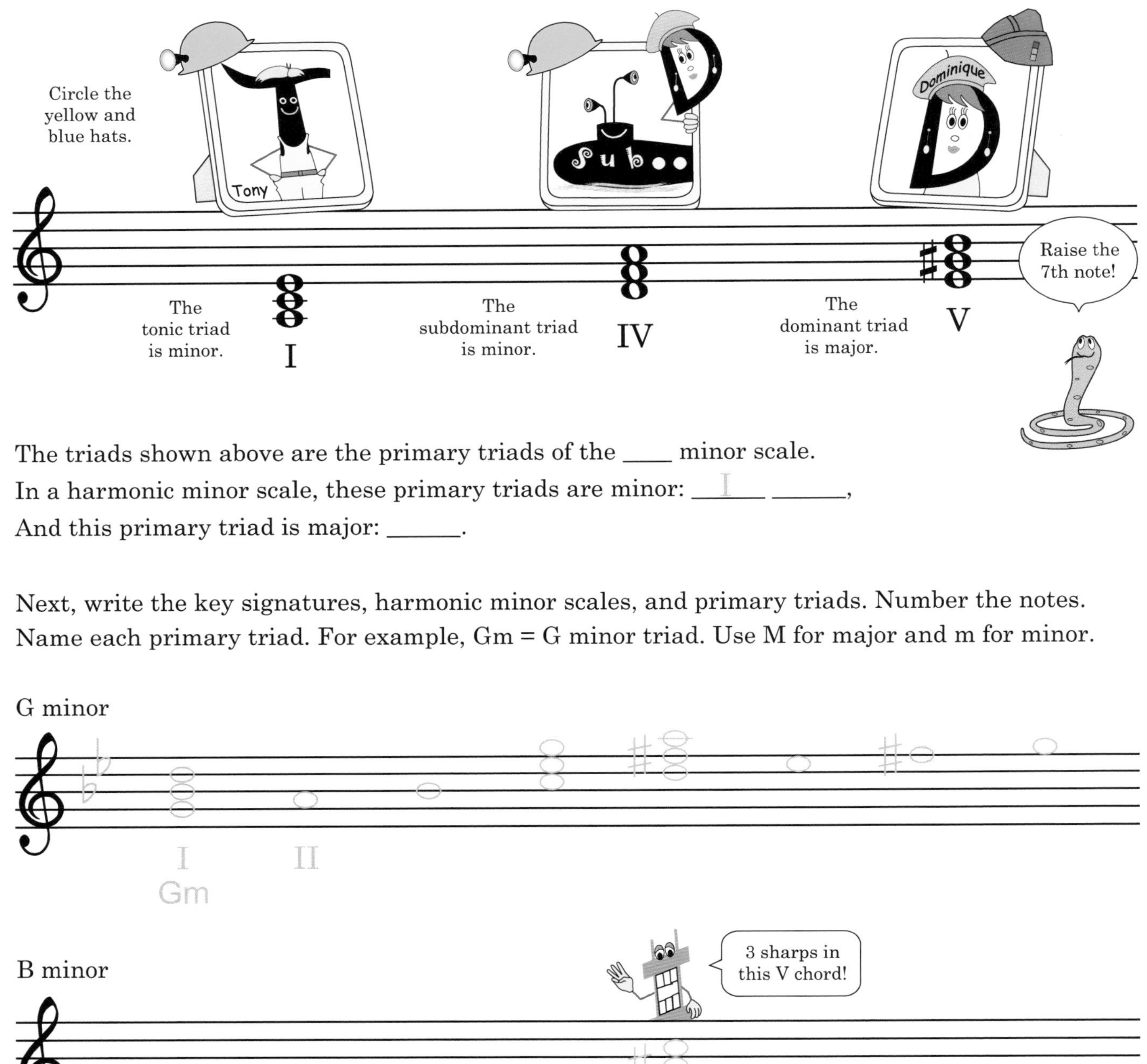

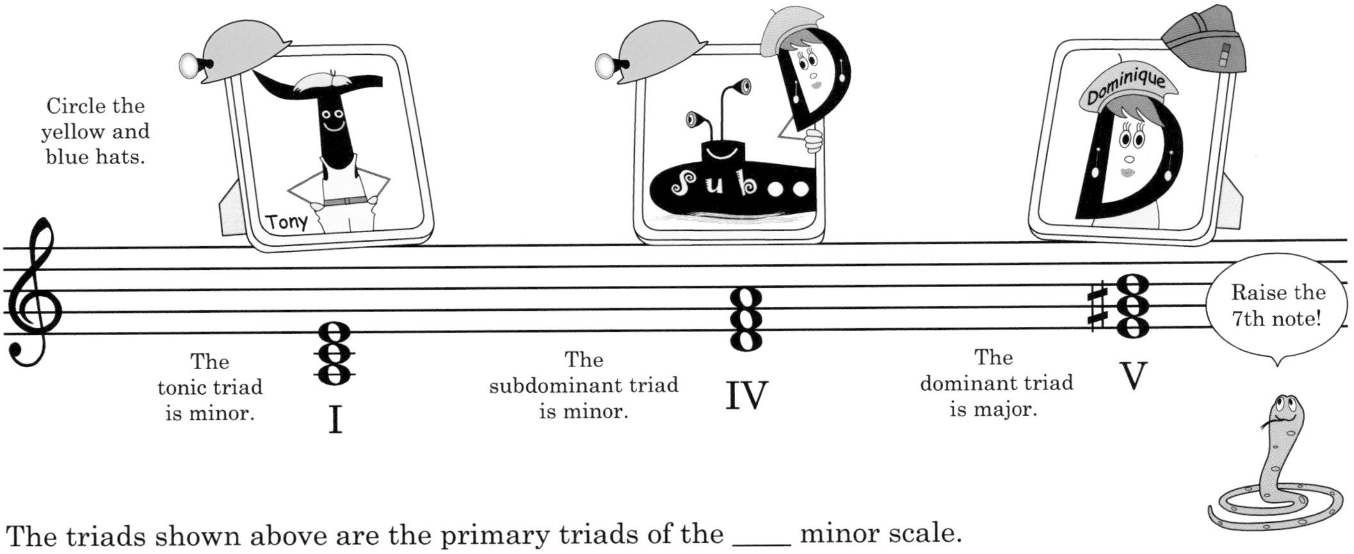
Circle the yellow and blue hats.
Tony
Sub
Dominique
Raise the 7th note!
The tonic triad is minor.
I
The subdominant triad is minor.
IV
The dominant triad is major.
V

The triads shown above are the primary triads of the ____ minor scale.
In a harmonic minor scale, these primary triads are minor: __I___ ______,
And this primary triad is major: ______.

Next, write the key signatures, harmonic minor scales, and primary triads. Number the notes.
Name each primary triad. For example, Gm = G minor triad. Use M for major and m for minor.

G minor

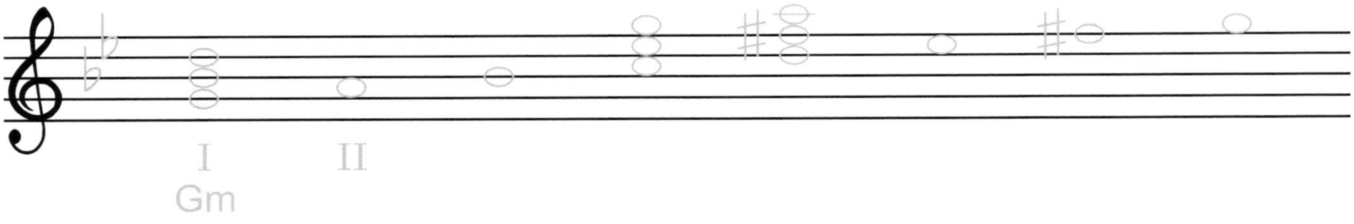
I
II
Gm

B minor

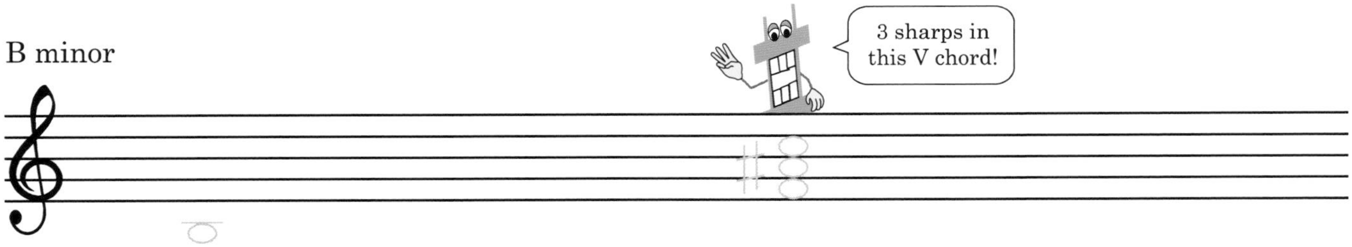
3 sharps in this V chord!

E minor

2 sharps in this V chord!

Doctor Mozart Music Theory Workbook, Level 2C. © MMVIII, MMXIII Machiko and Paul Christopher Musgrave. Published by April Avenue Music. www.DoctorMozart.com 800 567-8878

How Long Are Dotted Quarter Notes?

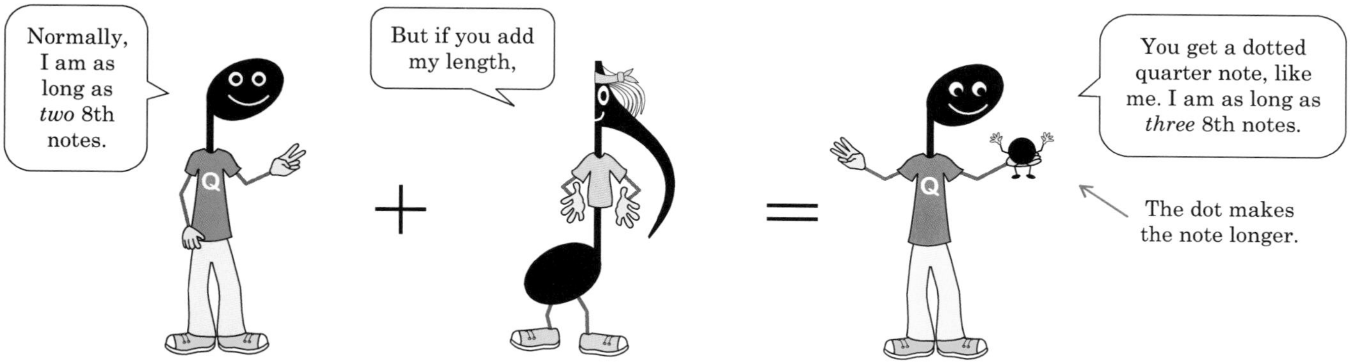
Normally, I am as long as *two* 8th notes.
But if you add my length,
You get a dotted quarter note, like me. I am as long as *three* 8th notes.
The dot makes the note longer.

Answer with a single note.

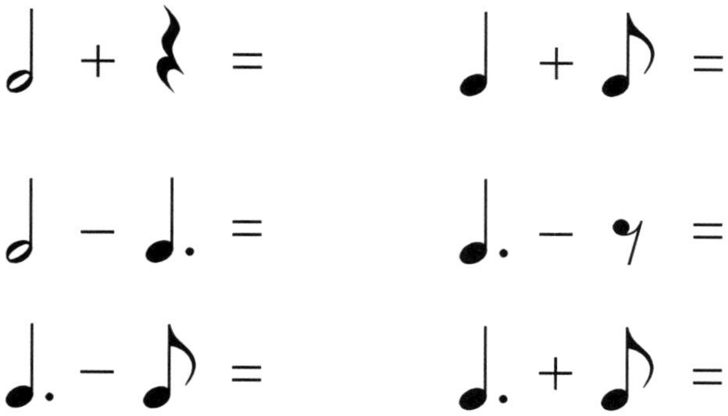

Tap this rhythm several times until you can do it well.

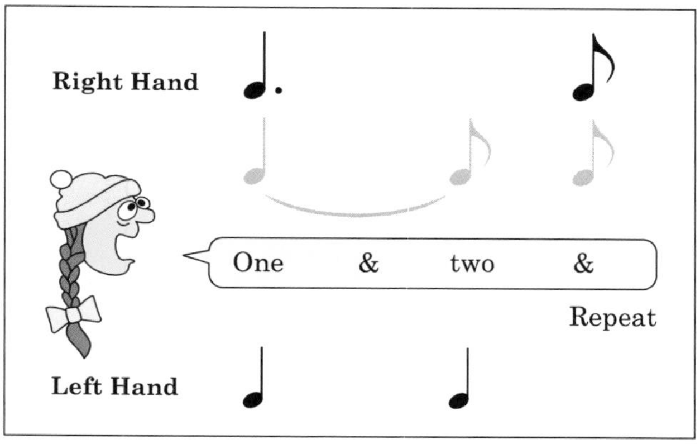
Right Hand
One & two &
Repeat
Left Hand

The top notes have the same rhythm as the gray notes.

Write a note in each box to complete each bar. Number the beats.
Tap while counting aloud. Practice until you have mastered each rhythm.

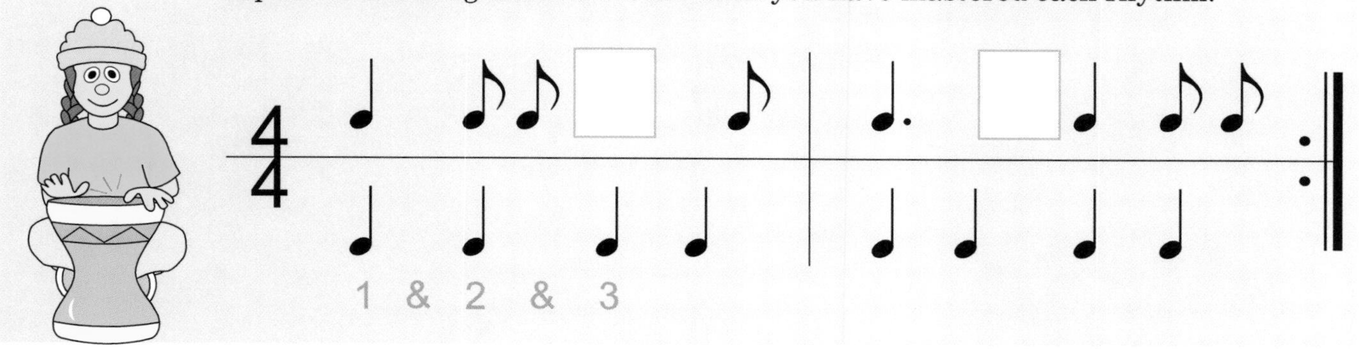
1 & 2 & 3

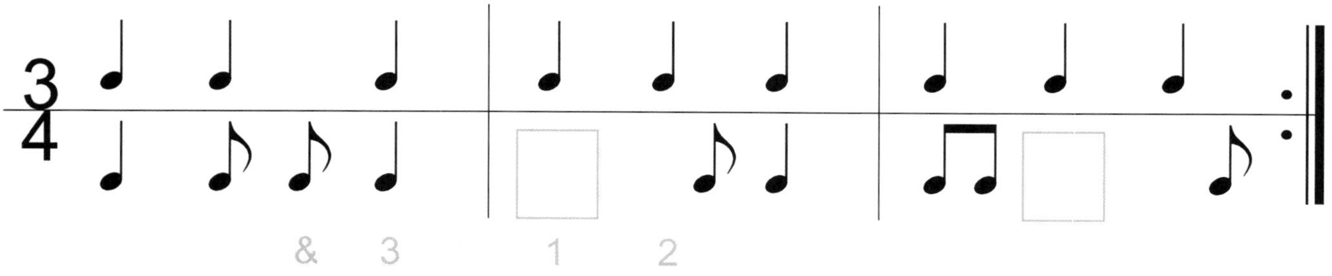
& 3 1 2

 © MMVIII, MMXIII Machiko and Paul Christopher Musgrave. Published by April Avenue Music. www.DoctorMozart.com 800 567-8878

Sixteenth Notes

A 16th note has two flags.
Here is how to draw a 16th note.

① Draw a quarter note.
② Add a flag.
③ Add a second flag.
Flags

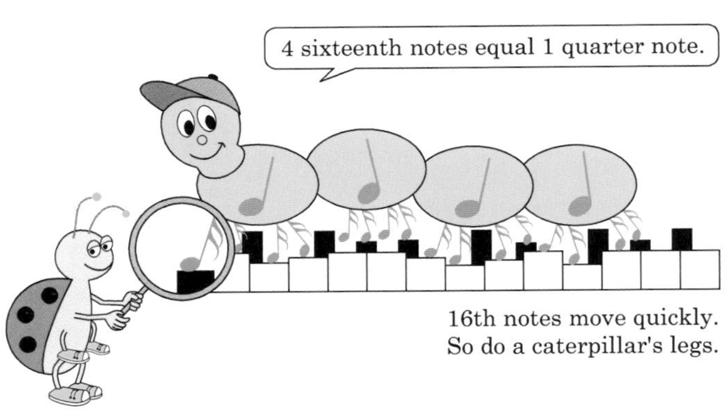

4 sixteenth notes equal 1 quarter note.

16th notes move quickly.
So do a caterpillar's legs.

Trace these notes.

Two sixteenth notes are as long as ____ eighth note.

Four sixteenth notes are as long as ____ quarter note.

For easier reading, adjacent 16th notes can be connected with beams.
Beams

Trace these notes.

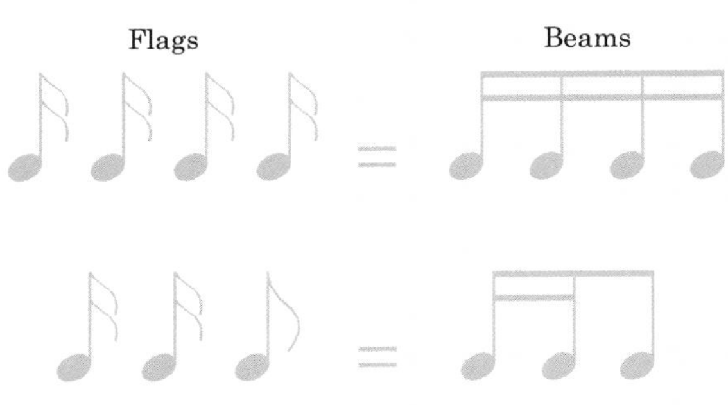

Flags
Beams

Connect 16th notes with a beam only if they are in the same beat.

Next, change the flags to beams. Change the beams to flags. Draw bar lines. Tap the rhythm.

2
4

Write a single note to complete each equation.

♪ + ♪ = ♩   ♩ + (beamed notes) =   ♩. − ♪ =

♪ − (16th note) =   ♪ + (16th note) + (16th note) =   (16th note) + (16th note) =

Sixteenth Rests

This is a sixteenth rest.
It tells you to stay silent for the length of a sixteenth note.

How to draw a 16th rest

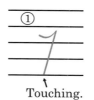

Draw an eighth rest. Make the stem touch the bottom line.
①
Touching.

Then add another flag in the 2nd space.
②
5
4
3
2
1

Fill these two bars with sixteenth and eighth rests. Count the beats.

1 - po - ta - to

Draw bar lines.

Answer with one rest.

= + + ____

− ____ =

+ + + = ____

= − ____

Write a single rest in each box to make the total duration in each box one quarter note.

8th and 16th Notes and Rests

Write *rests* to ensure that the total duration in each box is one quarter note.

Write *notes* to ensure that the total duration in each box is one quarter note.

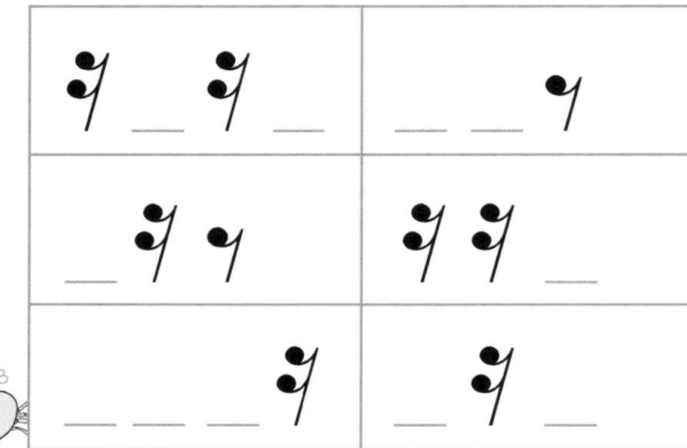

Complete each equation with a single rest.

25 cents
25 cents

Next, write the correct clefs. Name each key signature as a minor key. Fill the bars with 8th and 16th notes and rests. Number the beats. Use an accidental to raise each leading note.

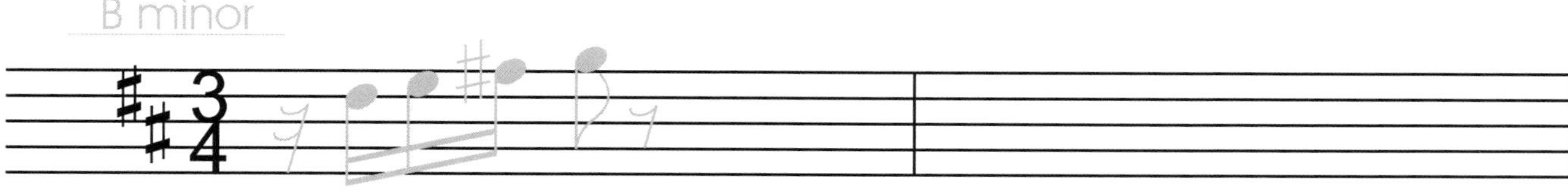

B minor

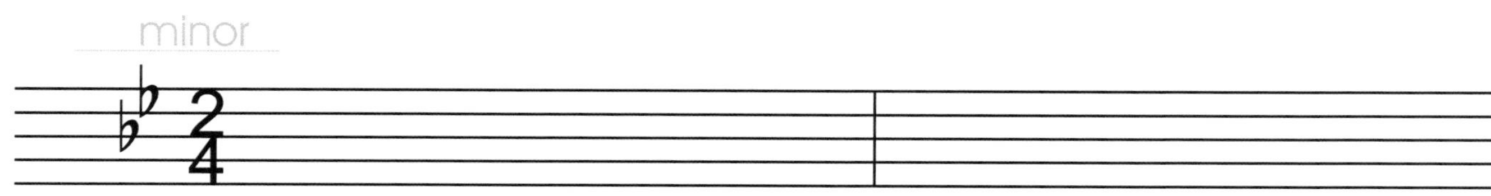

minor

  Published by April Avenue Music. www.DoctorMozart.com 800 567-8878

Scale Review

On each staff, write the correct key signature. Write a descending scale and the primary triads. Draw square and V brackets.

B♭ Major

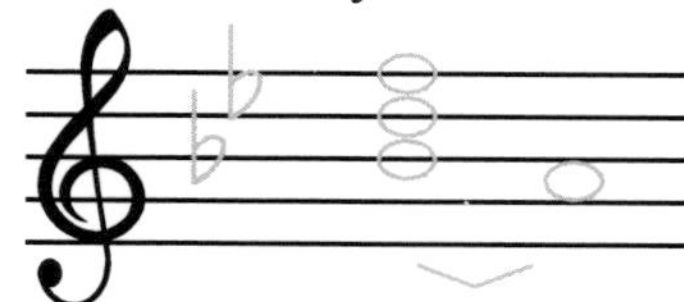

B harmonic minor

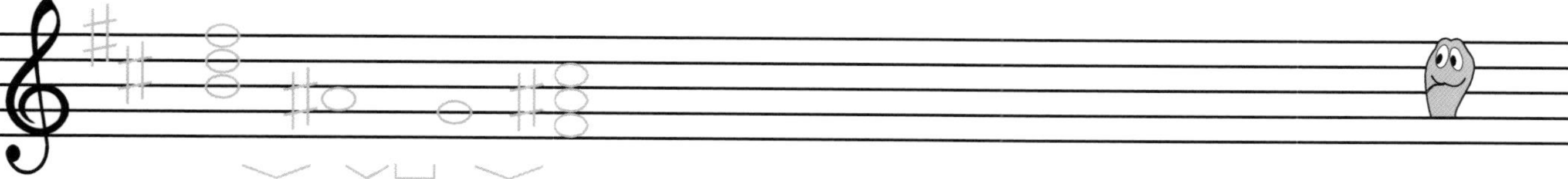

G harmonic minor

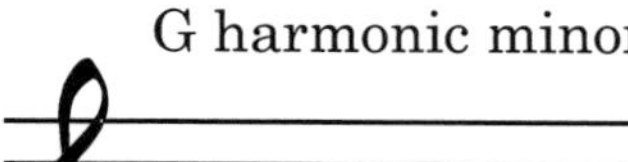

Name this scale. Circle any notes that do not belong in the G major scale.

Name this scale. Circle any notes that do not belong in the D major scale.

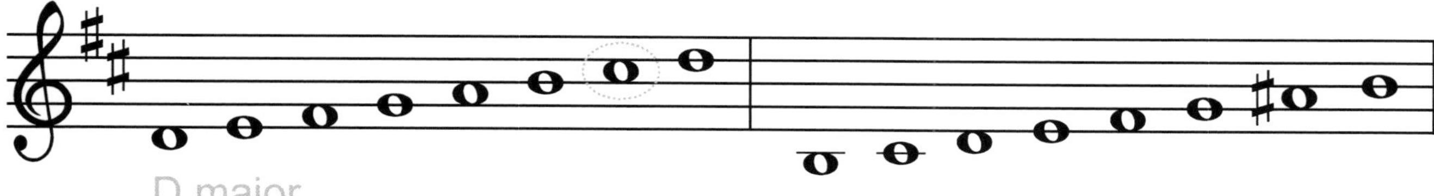
D major

Name this scale. Circle any notes that do not belong in the G major scale.

Name this scale. Circle any notes that do not belong in the E harmonic minor scale.

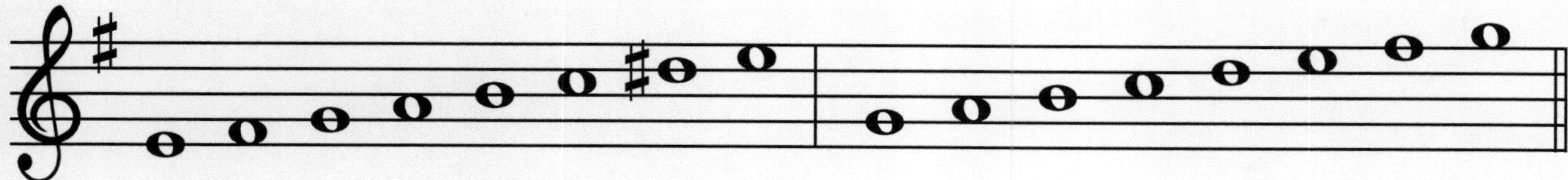

Name this scale. Circle any notes that do not belong in the F major scale.

Name this scale. Circle any notes that do not belong in the B flat major scale.

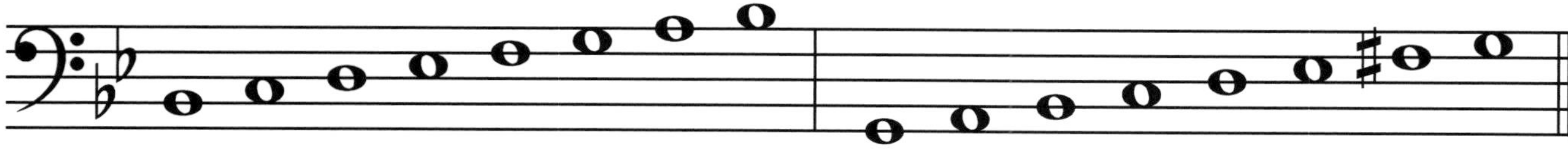

Chord Quiz

Primary Triads
IV I V

Each printed note is the tonic of a harmonic minor scale. Write the key signatures. Write the primary triads.

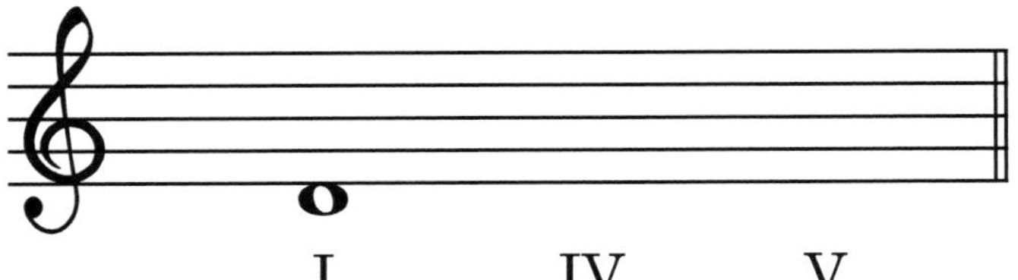
I IV V

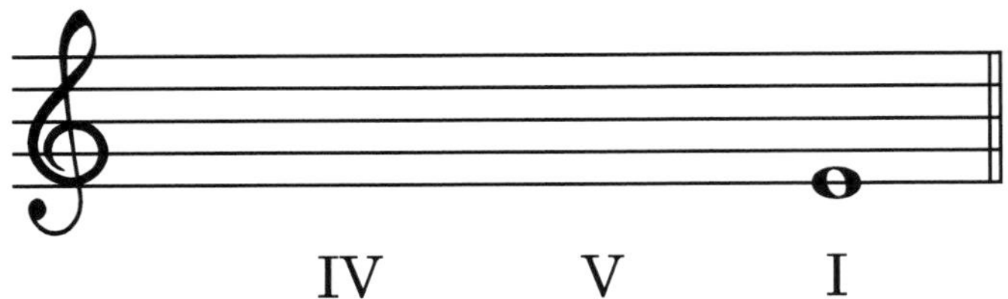
IV V I

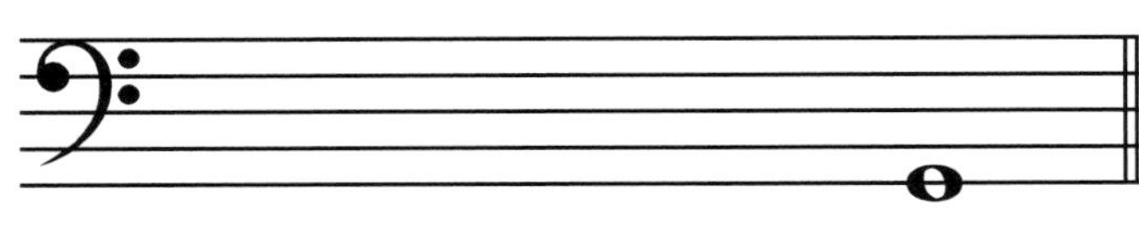
V IV I

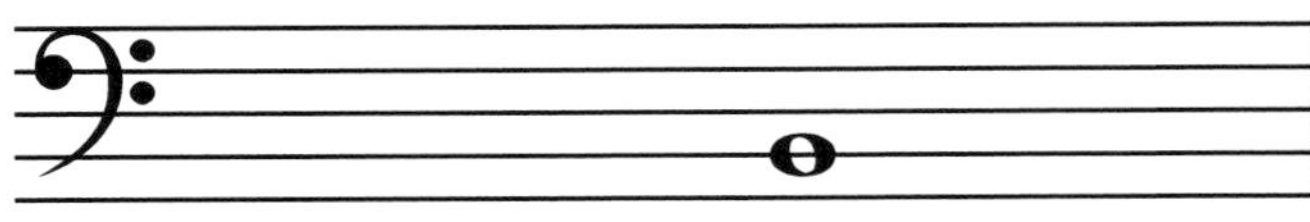
IV I V

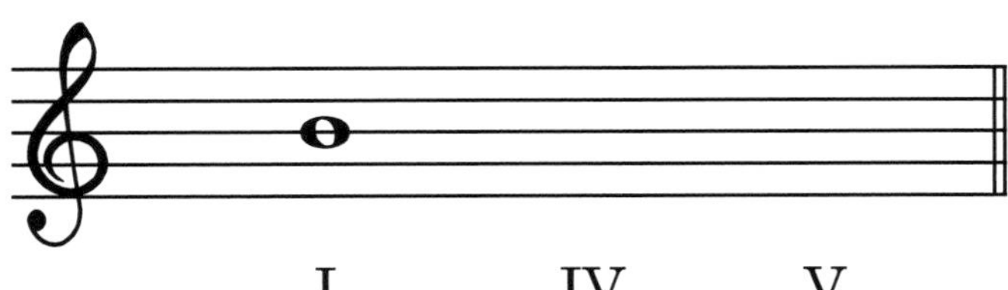
I IV V

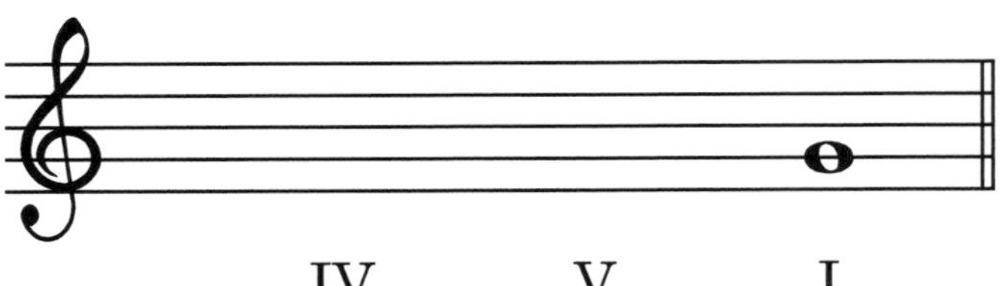
IV V I

Next, some of these triads belong to more than one scale. Under each triad, write a Roman numeral to indicate the triad's position in each scale. If it does not belong, write an X.

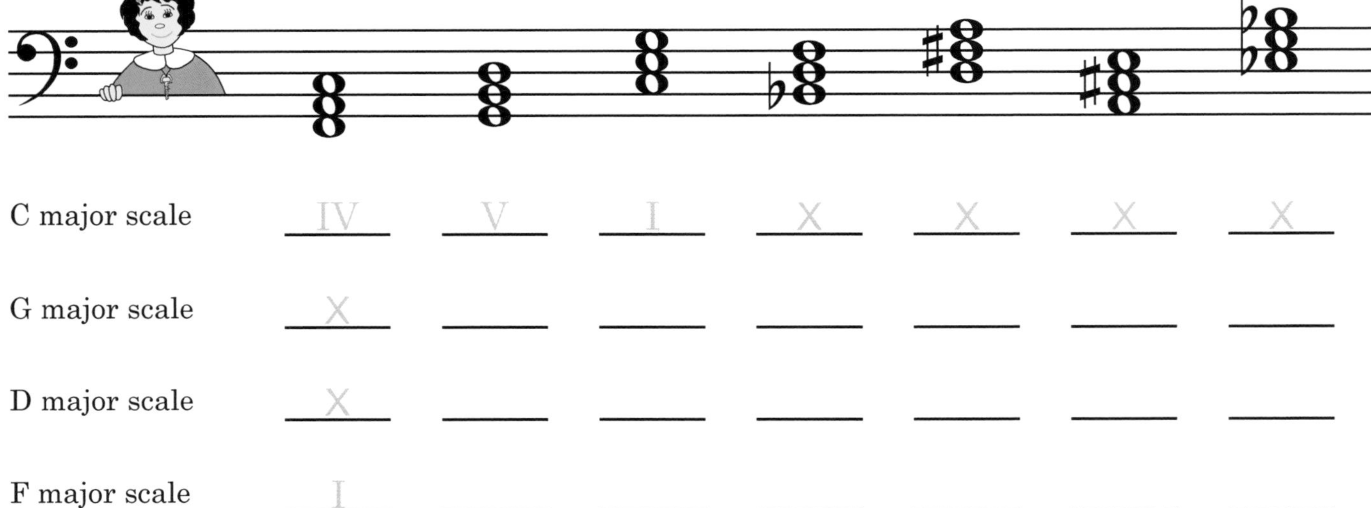
Chords & keys.

C major scale	IV	V	I	X	X	X	X
G major scale	X						
D major scale	X						
F major scale	I						
B flat major scale	V						

  Published by April Avenue Music. www.DoctorMozart.com 800 567-8878

Certificate of Achievement
Congratulations!
Student name
Now that you have completed
Doctor Mozart Music Theory
Workbook Level 2C,
you are ready for Level 3.
Teacher
Date
Dr. Mozart

  Published by April Avenue Music. www.DoctorMozart.com 800 567-8878

CPSIA information can be obtained
at www.ICGtesting.com
Printed in the USA
LVIC05n2240250913
354113LV00004B
9780978127794